FIDEL CASTRO'S POLITICAL STRATEGY

Fidel Castro's Political Strategy

FROM MONCADA TO VICTORY
by Marta Harnecker

with

History Will Absolve Me
by Fidel Castro

Pathfinder   NEW YORK   LONDON   MONTREAL   SYDNEY

ISBN 0-87348-666-8 paper; ISBN 0-87348-665-X cloth
Library of Congress Catalog Card Number 87-61469

Manufactured in the United States of America
First edition, 1987 • Third printing, 1997

Pathfinder
410 West Street, New York, NY 10014, U.S.A.
Fax: (212) 727-0150
CompuServe: 73321,414
Internet: pathfinder@igc.apc.org

PATHFINDER DISTRIBUTORS AROUND THE WORLD:
Australia (and Asia and the Pacific):
        Pathfinder, 19 Terry St., Surry Hills, Sydney, N.S.W. 2010
        Postal address: P.O. Box K879, Haymarket, N.S.W. 2000
Canada:
        Pathfinder, 4581 rue St-Denis, Montreal, Quebec, H2J 2L4
Iceland:
        Pathfinder, Klapparstíg 26, 2d floor, 101 Reykjavík
        Postal address: P. Box 233, 121 Reykjavík
New Zealand:
        Pathfinder, La Gonda Arcade, 203 Karangahape Road,
        Auckland • Postal address: P.O. Box 8730, Auckland
Sweden:
        Pathfinder, Vikingagatan 10, S-113 42, Stockholm
United Kingdom (and Europe, Africa except South Africa, and
        Middle East): Pathfinder, 47 The Cut, London, SE1 8LL
United States (and Caribbean, Latin America, and South Africa):
        Pathfinder, 410 West Street, New York, NY 10014

Contents

Fidel Castro's Political Strategy

From Moncada to Victory

by Marta Harnecker

" . . . history can
be made but it
cannot be
falsified . . . "
— Fidel Castro

Introduction

My aim in this work is to analyze the chief characteristics of Fidel Castro's political strategy for building the bloc of social forces that enabled him to defeat Batista and the oligarchical, proimperialist regime that supported him. This opened the way for building socialism in Cuba and, in so doing, transformed the Caribbean island into the beacon of the oppressed peoples of the Americas.

I have discussed other aspects of Castro's political strategy in my books *La revolución social (Lenin y América Latina)* (The social revolution: Lenin and Latin America) (Managua: Editorial Nueva Nicaragua, 1986) and *Instrumentos leninistas de dirección política* (Leninist tools of political leadership) (in preparation).

My purpose is to provide revolutionaries in the Americas with an overall view of Fidel Castro's skilled, flexible political leadership, based chiefly on the letters and speeches of the central leader of the Cuban revolution. However, his political and military strategy, including the way in which the revolutionary vanguard was built, deserves further study.

I am grateful to Mario Mencía for his advice on history and to all those whose critical views helped me to improve this book.

Marta Harnecker
Havana,
November 7, 1985

(Note: Most of the letters quoted in the book are from Fidel Castro's personal files in the Office of Historic Affairs of the Council of State of the Republic of Cuba. Reference to them will be abbreviated OHA.)

The July 26 Movement and the Orthodox Party

It was at Havana University that Fidel Castro, son of a wealthy farming family and future leader of the Cuban revolution, acquired a revolutionary outlook. At the time he belonged to a non-Marxist party, the Cuban People's Party, popularly known as the Orthodox Party.

Its program, mainly reflecting the interests of the radical, anti-imperialist middle class, called for nationalistic measures against the United States monopolies. The Orthodox Party also put special emphasis on measures against corruption in government. It was a populist, multiclass party made up mainly of workers, farmers, and middle-class people, under bourgeois leadership.[1]

The party's popularity was mainly due to the extraordinary charisma of its undisputed leader, Eduardo Chibás,[2] who had become known during the student struggles of the twenties and the battles against the dictatorship that followed. A fiery debater, Chibás headed a movement for civic and moral reform that was deeply rooted in the masses.

The highly heterogeneous Orthodox Party included a "left wing" made up largely of university students. Among them were Fidel and most of the leaders of the group of young people who in 1953 would attack the Moncada garrison. These youth knew something about scientific socialism and had an advanced political awareness, which Fidel would describe some years later as a "Marxist political framework" with deep roots in Cuban traditions, especially in the ideas of José Martí.[3]

In 1973, on the twentieth anniversary of the Moncada attack, the Cuban leader said in regard to that time in his life: "Martí taught us his ardent patriotism, his impassioned love for freedom, dignity, and honor of man, his repudiation of despotism, and his boundless faith in the people. . . .

"Céspedes gave us the splendid example of beginning with just a handful of men, when conditions were ripe for it, a war that would last ten years.

"Agramonte, Maceo, Gomez, and other leaders of our struggles for independence showed us the courage and fighting spirit of our people, irregular warfare, and the possibilities of adapting forms of popular armed struggle to the features of the terrain and to enemy superiority in numbers and weapons."[4]

He went on to point out the contributions they received from Marxism:

"The class concept of a society as divided between exploiters and exploited; the materialist conception of history; bourgeois relations of production as the final antagonistic form of social production; the inevitable advent of a classless society as the result of the development of the productive forces under capitalism and of the social revolution. . . .

"Marxism taught us," he added, "above all about the historic mission of the working class, the only truly revolutionary class, the class called upon to transform capitalist society to its very foundation, and about the role of the masses in the revolution.

"Lenin's *State and Revolution* enlightened us about the role of the state as the tool for domination of the oppressor classes and the need to create a revolutionary power capable of crushing the resistance of the exploiters."

He concluded by saying:

"The basic nucleus of leaders of our movement . . . regarded Marxism-Leninism as the only rational and scientific conception of revolution and the only method for fully understanding the situation of our own country."[5]

In August 1951, Chibás, who was beginning to become discredited in the eyes of the public because of his failure to come up with evidence to back up his charge of corruption against a top government official, became severely depressed. This led him to an extreme act during one of his regular radio broadcasts: he attempted suicide while on the air, a final effort to shake up the consciousness of the people, calling on them to fight for economic and political independence.[6]

Following the death of the outstanding Orthodox leader, Fidel found himself a member of a party with a very broad popular base, but without a consistent political leadership. The official Orthodox leaders were reformists who managed well within the system.[7]

At that time there was a party that was ideologically closer to Fidel's Marxist conceptions, but its membership was very small, primarily due to the fierce anticommunist campaign of the cold war period. This was the Popular Socialist Party (Communist Party).[8]

Taking these facts into account, the young law student decided to use his leadership qualities working with the Orthodox membership. Among the Orthodox youth, especially those of humble background, he recruited the future cadres of the new type of revolutionary vanguard, which he already had in mind. Those who joined the new organization were unknown. None of the official Orthodox Party leaders was recruited.[9]

Even though Marxist cadres made up a majority of the leadership nucleus of the new organization, they did not use Marxist terminology in their political speeches.

Fidel began to work out a strategy for leading the masses influenced by the Orthodox Party toward revolutionary positions. Even before Batista's March 10, 1952, coup,[10] which ended half a century of Cuba's republican existence, he realized that power could not be won in the traditional way, by means of elections. Instead it would have to be taken "in a revolutionary way." But because the period was one of parliamentary freedoms, he set out to make use of the platform offered by elections to "propose a revolutionary program around which to mobilize the masses and advance toward the revolutionary seizure of power."[11]

However, once the March 10, 1952, military coup closed off all constitutional avenues, a change in tactics became necessary. The Orthodox Party fell into disarray, splitting into several tendencies. Desperation and confusion prevailed among the membership. In the midst of this, the young Orthodox members led by Fidel began preparations for attacking the Moncada garrison in Santiago as the only way to take power under the new conditions created by the Batista dictatorship.

An intensive recruitment drive was carried out. By July 1953 the movement had at least 1,500 people trained and organized in some 150 cells. Nonetheless, because of the scarcity of arms, only 151 militants took an active part in the attack.

Fewer than ten people knew the exact target ahead of time. Preparations for the attack were carried out in a highly compartmentalized fashion. Raúl Castro himself learned that the action would take place in Oriente Province only "when he and other *compañeros* were given their train tickets and saw they were headed for Santiago.

"With the exception of those who did the driving, the people who traveled by car didn't even know what province they were headed for. Only when guns and uniforms were distributed shortly before departure for the action early on the morning of July 26 did they find out just what 'the plan' was."[12]

The intention was not at all to seize "revolutionary power with a handful of men," Fidel emphasized in analyzing the action in December 1961. "We never had any such idea. Our entire revolutionary strategy was bound up with a revolutionary conception; that is, we knew that power could be seized only with the support of the people, with the mobilization of the masses."[13]

Eight years after the abortive attempt to topple Batista, Raúl Castro, one of the participants, explained its significance in greater detail.

"It was not a putsch designed to score an easy victory without the masses. It was a surprise action to disarm the enemy and arm the people, with the aim of beginning armed revolutionary action.

"It was not an action intended solely to remove Batista and his gang from power. It marked the start of action to transform Cuba's entire political, economic, and social system and put an end to the foreign oppression, poverty, unemployment, ill health, and ignorance that weighed upon our country and our people."

He recognized that "at the time Fidel did not have an organization corresponding to those plans and committed to carrying them out. . . . He trusted that, in view of the political situation in the country and the existing discontent, fighters would come forward spontaneously as soon as there were guns and people ready to launch and lead the action. However, what needs to be stressed is that the action was organized not behind the backs of the masses, but in order to obtain the means of arming the masses and mobilizing them for armed struggle. The idea was not to seize the seat of government and grab power, but to launch revolutionary action to lead the people to power. . . .

"We agreed, we understood, that a mass movement would have to be launched to destroy the dictatorship," Raúl Castro added. "However, given the existing factors, how could that be achieved? Around that time Fidel used to say: we have to start up a small engine to help start up the big engine. . . . The small engine would be the capture of the Moncada fortress, the one farthest from the capital, the one which, once we held it, would trigger the big engine, the people fighting, with the weapons we would seize, for the laws and measures, the program that we would proclaim. . . .

"The Moncada attack was not an action aimed just at the overthrow of the dictatorship, much less one that ignored the country's economic and social plight.

"It was based precisely on the people's complete rejection of Batista, his government, and all it stood for. The general crisis of our semicolonial structure was worsening. Unemployment was climbing. The workers, the farmers, all the popular sectors of our country were discontented. Even our capitalist class was very dissatisfied because of our economic stagnation and the ruinous competition it faced from the greedy Yankee imperialist monopolies, who were not overly concerned about the [discontent of the] capitalists because they knew the latter were paralyzed by their fear, especially in Latin America, that the working class and the farmers would head the patriotic and democratic struggle and conquer power. The Yankee imperialist monopolies were confident that in the crisis, the national capitalist class would align itself with them against Cuban sovereignty and independence."[14]

Fidel would state many years later that the spectacular action had three goals: "First, to paralyze the activities of the traditional politicians, who were trying to resolve the situation by making deals and arranging a nonrevolutionary electoral compromise; second, to lift the people's revolutionary spirit; and third, to gather the minimum resources required" for carrying forward the revolutionary movement.[15]

In drawing up a balance sheet on the action, Fidel said that the first two objectives had been correct. But in regard to the third, experience showed that there had been no need to make "so much noise." The force that assaulted Moncada could easily have captured the garrison in Bayamo, near the Sierra Maestra. That would have provided the attackers with guns for eighty-two fighters, much more than the revolutionaries had several years later when they launched the guerrilla struggle in that area after the *Granma* landing.[16]

The forces attacking Moncada planned to seize radio stations and urge the people to rise up against Batista, broadcasting Eduardo Chibás's last speech over and over again, thereby "providing immediate proof," said Fidel, "of a revolutionary explosion completely independent of the politicians of the past. . . .

"Had our revolutionary effort been victorious, our aim was to place power in the hands of the most committed members of the Orthodox Party.

"The restoration of the 1940 constitution, adapted, of course, to the abnormal situation, was the first point in our proclamation to the people. Once we held the capital of Oriente we would have promulgated six basic laws with deep revolutionary content. These would have provided the small sugarcane growers, tenant farmers, sharecroppers, and squatters with definitive possession of the land, with the state paying compensation to those hurt by the law. Workers would have been granted the right to a share in company profits. Sugarcane growers would have been assigned 55 percent of the revenues from the sugar produced from their cane. (These measures would naturally have been coordinated with a dynamic, energetic government policy, including direct intervention in the creation of new industries through the mobilization of the large reserves of national capital, thereby breaking the organized resistance of powerful interests).

"Another proposed law would have dismissed from office all municipal, provincial, and national judicial and administrative officials who had betrayed the constitution by swearing loyalty to [Batista's] statutes. Finally, one law called for the confiscation of all the property of all the corrupt officeholders of the past, following a speedy investigation."[17]

At that time Fidel saw his organization as an integral part of the Orthodox masses, impelling them into action. This would in turn inspire the people as a whole. He explained this three years later, in August 1955, in a message sent from exile to the Congress of Orthodox Activists. "The July 26 Revolutionary Movement," he wrote, "does not constitute a tendency within the party: it is the revolutionary apparatus of Chibás's followers. It is rooted in the masses, from which it sprang to fight the dictatorship when the Orthodox Party lay helpless, broken into a thousand pieces. We have never abandoned his ideas, we have remained loyal to the purest principles of the great fighter whose death we commemorate today. . . ."

That message, which proclaimed a revolutionary line, was adopted unanimously by the five hundred representatives at the congress. Not one of the reformist official leaders of the Orthodox Party took the floor to speak against it.

That afforded convincing proof, according to Fidel Castro, that the "immense majority of the party's rank and file, the best of its membership," followed the July 26 line.[18]

When he broke with the Orthodox leadership on March 19, 1956,[19] due to their shameful behavior in betraying the revolutionary line of the party by seeking to cut a deal with Batista, he declared:

"It is not our fault if the country has been led into an abyss from which it can be saved only by revolution. We do not love force. Because we hate force we are not willing to be governed through force. We do not love violence. Because we hate violence, we are not willing to continue to put up with the violence that has been used against the nation for the past four years.

"Now the struggle belongs to the people. The July 26 Movement was organized and strengthened to aid the people in their heroic struggle to recover the freedoms and rights that were taken from them.

"July 26 against March 10!

"The masses who follow Chibás do not regard the July 26 Movement as something apart from Orthodoxism. It is Orthodoxism without a leadership of estate owners like Fico Fernández Casas, without sugar plantation owners like Gerardo Vázquez; without stock-market speculators, without magnates of industry and commerce, without attorneys for the big interests, without provincial political bosses, without corrupt politicians of any kind. The best of Orthodoxism is waging this beautiful struggle together with us.

"And to Eduardo Chibás we will pay the only homage worthy of his life and self-sacrifice: the freedom of his people, which those who have done nothing but shed crocodile tears on his grave will never be able to offer.

"The July 26 Movement is the revolutionary organization of the humble, by the humble, and for the humble.

"The July 26 Movement is the hope of redemption for the Cuban working class, to whom the political cliques have nothing to offer. It is the hope of land for the people of the countryside who live like pariahs in the homeland that their grandparents fought to free. It is the hope of return for the emigrés who had to leave their country because they could not work or live in it. It is the hope of bread for the hungry and of justice for the forsaken.

"The July 26 Movement makes its own the cause of all those who have been killed in the harsh struggle since March 10, 1952. We proclaim calmly before the nation, before their wives, children, parents, and sisters and brothers, that the revolution will never compromise with their tormentors.

"The July 26 Movement is a warm invitation to close ranks, extended with open arms to all the revolutionaries of Cuba, without petty partisan differences, regardless of what differences there may have been in the past.

"The July 26 Movement is the healthy, just future of our country, it is honor pledged before the people, the promise that will be kept."[20]

To sum up: What marked Fidel Castro's strategy in the building of the vanguard of the revolutionary process is the absolute conviction that there can be no revolution without the masses of the people.

Objective Conditions for the Revolution and the Role of the Vanguard

At the same time, however, Fidel was deeply convinced that many if not all of the objective conditions for revolution were present in his country, and that the role of the vanguard was not to create these conditions but to speed up the growth in awareness of the masses.

The people's only way out of their desperate plight was to support a movement that aimed at radically changing the existing political situation by adopting a series of revolutionary measures.

Some analysts have misinterpreted certain quotes from the Cuban revolutionary leader, taking them out of their context. They have claimed that the July 26 Movement fell into a voluntarist deviation because it sought to "create" conditions for the revolution without waiting for them to mature within Cuban society.

To be sure, in a December 1, 1961, television appearance, Fidel did say: "It seemed to us that revolutionary conditions had to be created, and they had to be created through struggle."[21] However, he clarified this formulation further on: "There cannot be a revolution in the first place unless there are objective circumstances that at a given time in history facilitate the revolution and make it possible. That is, revolution cannot spring from men's minds."[22]

The interpretation mentioned above is not far from the position adopted by the Popular Socialist Party (PSP) toward the armed actions organized by Fidel and his group on July 26, 1953. At the time, the PSP was totally unaware of the deep motivations behind the Moncada action.

The PSP's *Carta Semanal* (Weekly letter) of October 20, 1953 — while defending the moral integrity and the honesty of the Moncada fighters — called the action an attempted "putsch" and a "desperate action which may be regarded as an adventure." Such actions, it held, "lead only to failure, the squandering of forces, and useless death."[23]

The PSP counterposed mass struggle to armed action. It was not capable of realizing that at the time conditions for combining different forms of struggle already existed, and that the people could participate not only in struggles around particular demands but also in armed struggle.

But Fidel had the ability to map out a strategy that, on the basis of the actual situation — in which objective conditions existed, although they were not yet fully developed — would lead in a very short time to optimum revolutionary results.

We should make it clear that when Fidel speaks of objective conditions he is thinking mainly, as will be seen in the following quotations, of what has come to be known as structural crisis.[24] This refers to a situation in which the existing economic and repressive conditions make life increasingly unbearable for the masses, although they might not be fully aware of the reasons.

"We simply thought of a way to take advantage of the objective conditions existing in our country: in the first place, the existing system of exploitation . . . the situation of the rural people. . . . It never would have occurred to us to launch revolutionary struggle in a country where there were no big estate owners. That is, a revolutionary guerrilla struggle in the rural areas in a country without big estate owners, in a country where the farmers owned their land, in a country where there were cooperative farms and people's farms and where there was full employment for all — that never would have occurred to us.

"In our country everyone knows what the conditions in the countryside were. Among the peasants, those who weren't squatters were tenants. Squatters on government lands were constantly being victimized by eviction and other sorts of harassment. Sugarcane workers found harvest work for three or four months, and in the dead season, the rest of the year, they worked for two or three months more. Unemployment in the countryside was extremely high. Rural people were forced to head for the city, but there was unemployment there, too.

"Then there were the tenant farmers. Coffee growers who were tenants had to pay a third or a fourth of their crop. The tobacco tenant farmers, the sharecroppers, also had to pay 25 or 30 percent of their crop. The cane growers paid a lower percentage but it was still high in terms of the gross worth of the cane: they had to pay at least 5 percent of the gross worth of the cane.

"Farmers were the victims of all kinds of extortion and speculation. They were paid low prices for their crops. The speculators took advantage of the farmers' special plight to exploit them miserably. Products farmers had to buy in the countryside were sold at very high prices, while they received very low prices for their crops. That's the way things were in the countryside. The coffee growers lived up in the mountains. Who picked the coffee? Tens of thousands of men and women from the canefields, from the sugar plantations, who were out of work in the dead season, headed for the mountains to pick coffee.

"Coffee was grown in the mountains because the peasants who had been forced off the land by the sugar plantation owners and big cattle ranchers had sought a haven in the mountains and planted coffee there. It wasn't that coffee could grow only in the mountains, but because that was the corner where they could survive.

Further on Fidel summed up the objective conditions that led to the launching of the struggle at that time:

"We began that struggle on the basis of a series of assumptions, assumptions that were accurate. That is, assumptions about the existing social system of exploitation in our country and the conviction that our people wanted a revolutionary change. Even though that desire may not have been a fully conscious one, it certainly existed. People expressed it in their overall discontent, in the fact that a banner of rebellion immediately found support in broad sectors of the people. The people expressed their rebellious spirit and their political consciousness despite all the confusionism, all the propaganda, and all the lies by imperialism and reaction.

"We started from that assumption. It was accurate, and because it was, the hopes and the possibilities that we had envisioned came true. The lesson of this is that there cannot be a revolution in the first place unless there are objective circumstances that at a given time in history facilitate the revolution and make it possible.

"In other words, revolutions do not spring from the minds of men. . . . We can interpret a law of history, a given moment in historic development. Coming up with a correct interpretation means carrying forward the revolutionary movement. In Cuba our role was one of carrying forward that movement on the basis of understanding a set of objective conditions."[25]

In Cuba, the economic situation was critical, as in all dependent countries, with mounting long-term unemployment, a deplorable situation for the landless farmers who were either ruined or evicted, a decline in real wages, deficits in the trade balance, and huge losses to the country due to the reduction in the United States sugar quota in recent years. But concretely it wasn't until the end of 1958 that a conjunctural economic crisis developed. In fact, mainly owing to the extraordinary increase in the price of sugar on the world market, 1957 proved to be a prosperous year.

The situation changed near the end of 1958. For one thing, the price of sugar took a considerable plunge with the inevitable economic consequences for a single-crop country like Cuba. And for another, the military successes of the Rebel Army — which by the end of 1958 had taken the war from the Sierra Maestra in the east to the central region — endangered the sugar harvest, which accounted for 60 percent of the value of Cuban exports.[26]

These factors created a conjunctural crisis. The sugar capitalists had only two options: oust Batista by supporting the guerrillas or ask for United States intervention. Because of factors that lie outside the scope of this work, they opted for the former, thereby accelerating the fall of the dictator.[27]

The successes of the Rebel Army also had an undeniable influence on the state of mind of the masses. In April 1958, a general strike call met with failure, mainly as the result of a relationship of forces that was still favorable to the existing regime. The situation changed after the Battle of Jigüe on July 21, 1958, which ended with a solid victory for the Rebel Army and marked the start of its all-out, conclusive counteroffensive.

By the end of December the fall of Batista was imminent. Entire provinces were cut off from the rest of the country. Whole units of the army had been destroyed. The collapse of the regime was evident to all. In that context, a far cry from the situation in April, the general strike called by Fidel January 1, after the flight of the dictator, with the aim of preventing a military coup behind the backs of the people, was completely successful.

The masses of the people, who may have appeared to superficial observers to be passive onlookers of the fighting in the mountains, became the decisive actors in the revolutionary victory.

An entire people, aroused, stormed the repressive agencies of the dictatorship, hunting down and arresting informers and torturers, and in the process, becoming a vast army.[28]

"In a matter of minutes, or rather of hours, to be more

exact," said Fidel, "the Rebel Army virtually dominated the revolution in the fighting areas and the people dominated it in the urban areas. And the workers backed the movement with an all-out general strike. . . .

"The people then were not the same as seven years before, or twenty years before. They were now a people who had gained a consciousness of struggle. A people whose spirit of rebellion had developed and who rallied around, not the discredited traditional parties, but a revolutionary movement. A people who gathered around a small nucleus of revolutionary fighters, a small revolutionary army. A people who developed, who withstood murders, tortures, all manner of injustice and who felt all these things very strongly. And they were a people who had been gaining their bearings, learning to be alert, who had been preparing for a revolution.

"And so, when they tried to snatch the January 1 revolutionary victory from the people, they found to their amazement that the people took to the streets. They found to their amazement that the Rebel columns surrounded and disarmed the troops and that all of a sudden, a real revolution had achieved victory on that historic day."[29]

He added further on:

"The guerrilla movement was a lit match in dry kindling, given the existing conditions in our country. Little by little the struggle became the struggle of all the people. The people, all of the people, were the actors in that struggle. The masses were the ones who decided the contest. . . .

"What factor had mobilized the masses? The guerrilla struggle became a factor that mobilized the masses, that sharpened the struggle and the repression, that sharpened the regime's contradictions. . . ."

From what we have seen up to this point, we can say that Fidel did not limit himself to noting that in Cuba conditions existed for making the revolution and to waiting for those conditions to ripen by themselves. Rather, from a vanguard position, he acted on the objective conditions themselves, sharpening the existing contradictions and creating new ones. In other words, his action helped the objective and subjective conditions to reach full maturity, which did in fact speed up the revolutionary process in the country.

Character of the Revolution and the Relationship Between Classes

Even before the Moncada attack, Fidel fully realized, as we have seen, that the goal had to be not merely toppling Batista but carrying out a revolution. That was why he always opposed both the assassination of the dictator and a military coup, two ways of eliminating Batista without changing the foundations of the system.

In addition, Fidel realized that the revolution of national liberation that he planned to begin was inseparable from a deep-going social revolution, that is, that the anti-imperialist revolutionary process had to end up being at the same time a socialist revolution.

Referring to this in his December 1, 1961, television appearance, he said:

"We had to make the anti-imperialist, socialist revolution.... The anti-imperialist, socialist revolution could only be one, one single revolution, because there is only one revolution. That is the great dialectical truth of humanity: imperialism and, standing against it, socialism."[30]

However, the July 26 Movement never insisted on the revolutionary measures it planned to implement because it realized that "emphasizing an entire series of reforms and revolutionary laws, given the conditions of the anti-Batista struggle, would have weakened the camp of the forces confronting the regime."[31]

Now let's look at the different factors that the principal leader of the Cuban revolution took into consideration in hammering out the strategy that would build a bloc of social forces capable of finishing off not only Batista but the entire economic and social system on which his power rested.

What were the existing class relations? Which social forces could carry forward the revolutionary process?

On the basis of an analysis of the objective conditions of his country's economic and political development — a dependent capitalist country with moderate industrial development and a working class of some magnitude, especially in the rural areas — Fidel distinguished three fundamental forces on the political scene.

First: the big landowners; "the big capitalist class and its declassed hangers-on, their gangsters, their *mujalistas*" (tool of reaction and imperialism inside the labor movement); "the reactionary clergy";[32] and the transnational corporations operating in Cuba.

All these well-off, conservative sectors of the nation had shamelessly paraded before Batista to offer him their support the day after the March 13, 1957, abortive attack on the Presidential palace staged by the Revolutionary Directorate in a bid to assassinate the dictator. That action ended with the slaughter of a large number of the group that had carried it out, including its central leader, José Antonio Echeverría.[33]

"Any oppressive regime, any dictatorship, any despotism" suited those "who live in comfort, the conservative elements of the nation," said Fidel in his speech in his own defense before the Emergency Tribunal in Santiago on October 16, 1953.[34] He added that they were capable of prostrating themselves "before the masters of the moment until they grind their foreheads into the ground."[35]

In the hands of these sectors were "all the financial resources, all the economic resources, the entire press, all the radio; that is, the big radio and TV stations, the big newspapers, the best printshops. . . . In addition . . . all the American magazines, all that imperialist literature. . . . They held all those resources in their hands, the economic resources . . . they were simply the lords and masters of the country. . . ."[36]

Second: the so-called "national bourgeoisie," that is, capitalist sectors having contradictions with imperialism. Fidel was convinced that, given conditions in Cuba and Latin America in general, that sector of the capitalist class could not head the struggle against oligarchy and imperialism. The experiences of Latin American revolutionary processes had sufficiently shown that, despite their contradictions with Yankee imperialism, when the time came they would prove unable to stand up to it because they are "paralyzed by fear of social revolution and frightened by the cry of the exploited masses." Thus, faced with the dilemma "imperialism or revolution," only the "most progressive layers" of that class would be willing to support the revolutionary process.[37]

And third: the only force capable of carrying forward the revolutionary process in a consistent way — the Cuban people.

In "History Will Absolve Me," Fidel described clearly what he meant by "the people":

"When we speak of struggle and we mention the people, we mean the vast unredeemed masses, those to whom everyone makes promises and who are deceived by all; we mean the people who yearn for a better, more dignified, and more just nation; those who are moved by ancestral aspirations of justice, for they have suffered injustice and mockery generation after generation; those who long for great and wise changes in all aspects of their life; people who, to attain those changes, are ready to give even the very last breath they have, when they believe in something or in someone, especially when they believe in themselves. . . .

"In terms of struggle, when we talk about people we're talking about the *six hundred thousand* Cubans without work, who want to earn their daily bread honestly without having to emigrate from their homeland in search of a livelihood; the *five hundred thousand* farm laborers who live in miserable shacks, who work four months of the year and starve the rest, sharing their misery with their children, who don't have an inch of land to till and whose existence would move any heart not made of stone; the *four hundred thousand* industrial workers and laborers whose retirement funds have been embezzled, whose benefits are being taken away, whose homes are wretched quarters, whose salaries pass from the hands of the boss to those of the moneylender, whose future is a pay reduction and dismissal, whose life is endless work and whose only rest is the tomb; the *one hundred thousand* small farmers who live and die working land that is not theirs, looking at it with the sadness of Moses gazing at the promised land, to die without ever owning it, who like feudal serfs have to pay for the use of their parcel of land by giving up a portion of its produce, who cannot love it, improve it, beautify it, nor plant a cedar or an orange tree on it because they never know when a sheriff will come with the rural guard to evict them from it; the *thirty thousand* teachers and professors who are so devoted, dedicated, and so necessary to the better destiny of future generations and who are so badly treated and paid; the *twenty thousand* small businessmen weighed down by debts, ruined by the crisis, and harangued by a plague of grafting and venal officials; the *ten thousand* young professional people: doctors, engineers, lawyers, veterinarians, school teachers, dentists, pharmacists, newspapermen, painters, sculptors, etc., who finish school with their degrees, anxious to work and full of hope, only to find themselves at a dead end, all doors closed to them, and where no ear hears their clamor or supplication. These are the people, the ones who know misfortune and, therefore, are capable of fighting with limitless courage!"[38]

Armed Road Only After Institutional Means are Exhausted

Earlier, we noted that Fidel turned to war only as the last resort. The armed struggle was launched only after Batista annulled the existing legality with his coup of March 10, 1952.

"We are not professional troublemakers nor are we blind proponents of violence. We would not resort to violence if the better homeland that we yearn for could be achieved with the weapons of reason and intelligence," he wrote in a document published in *Bohemia* magazine May 25, 1955, a few months before the Moncada prisoners were amnestied.

"No people would follow a group of adventurers who sought to plunge the country into civil strife unless injustice held sway, unless there were no peaceful, legal means provided to all the citizens in the civic battle of ideas. We agree with Martí that 'he who starts a war that can be avoided is a criminal, and so is he who fails to start a war that is inevitable.'

"The Cuban nation will never see us promoting a civil war that can be avoided. By the same token I repeat that whenever shameful circumstances like those that followed the March 10 coup occur in Cuba it will be a crime to fail to start the inevitable rebellion."[39]

After the fraudulent elections at the end of 1954, which transformed the dictator into a "constitutional" president, the regime made efforts to improve its image. With this in mind, Fidel decided when he left prison in May 1955 that the most important thing at that moment was to show that Batista's efforts were pure demagogy.

When Batista began his "legal" term on February 24, 1955, he had announced that the 1940 constitution would again be in force, as had been advocated by the Moncada heroes. He also announced that midterm congressional elections would be held within two years and general elections in four years. There was talk of plans for elections to a constitutional assembly that would modify the constitution.

The campaign for amnesty for the political prisoners had gained such momentum that Batista found it necessary to include all the Moncada fighters on the list. The climate in the country had awakened hopes for democratic solutions among the more backward sectors of the people. The great majority of the leaders of the capitalist parties had joined the game.

Fidel left prison in the midst of that climate of apparent democratization. Much to the surprise of many, his first words were not a call to armed struggle:

"We are in favor of a democratic solution. Only the regime has opposed peaceful solutions. The only way out of Cuba's current situation, as I see it, is immediate general elections. The constituent assembly business is a maneuver by the regime to elect Batista, through a prefabricated opposition, in another shameful November 1. It shouldn't be forgotten that we Cubans love peace, but we love liberty even more."[40]

"When we left prison, we already had a full strategy for struggle mapped out," he would explain several years after the victory of the revolution. "But in our opinion the most important thing at that time was to demonstrate that there was no political, that is, peaceful, solution of Cuba's plight with Batista in power. We had to show that to be the case in the eyes of the public. If the country was going to find itself forced into revolutionary violence, it would be the fault of the regime, not of the revolutionaries.

"So we said we were prepared to accept a peaceful solution on the basis of certain conditions, conditions we knew would never come about. It took only a few weeks to demonstrate to public opinion that Cuba's problems could never be solved peacefully, with Batista.

"[When and only when] that had been shown, in our judgment, did we resume preparations for armed struggle."[41]

Despite his intention of remaining in Cuba, seven weeks after his release from prison the hero of Moncada had to leave the country. Several of his closest comrades would soon follow.

The dictatorship was closing all the doors. It was frightened by the mounting repercussions among the masses of the denunciations of its crimes and the consistent criticism of the opportunistic, do-nothing line promoted by the political parties with the most popular support. Fidel was deprived of access to radio stations. Meetings at which he was scheduled to speak were banned. The newspaper *La Calle*, in which his articles were appearing, was closed down.[42]

"We have been left without ways to speak, write, hold public meetings, or make use of any civil rights," Fidel charged in his first manifesto from exile to the Cuban people, in August 1955.[43]

This was compounded by an atmosphere of slander, intimidation, and physical threats.

So, having exhausted all legal means, Fidel left Cuba to prepare to overthrow the dictatorship by revolutionary means. From exile he sent a message to the members of the Orthodox Party:

"The regime is in no way prepared to call immediate general elections, which all sectors of public opinion regard as the only formula for a peaceful solution of Cuba's tragedy. Much less will it do so in the face of a disarmed opposition that has failed to demonstrate its readiness to demand more forcefully the rights that have been stolen from the people. . . . Cuba thus finds itself at a crossroads. It is heading in the direction of the most shameful and hopeless political and moral prostration, which could last for twenty years, just as is the case in the Dominican Republic and in other countries of the Americas, unless it gloriously frees itself once and for all from oppression.

"One course consists of midterm elections, a deal with the regime, boundless ambitions for municipal posts and congressional seats, hunger, poverty, injustice, shame, betrayal of the people, criminal forgetting of the dead. The other course is *revolution*, the exercise of the right of the peoples to rise up against oppression; the historic continuation of the struggles of 1868, 1895, and 1933; ironclad intransigence against the treacherous March 10 coup and the shameful massacre of November; justice for the oppressed and hungry people; unselfishness, sacrifice, loyalty to the dead. There is no other option. The Orthodox ranks know that the time has come to choose one or the other."[44]

So important did Fidel regard the need for the masses to realize that all legal possibilities had been exhausted that just a few days before the *Granma* landing he decided to present Batista with an ultimatum. He told the progovernment daily *Alerta*:

"Unless there is a national solution within two weeks of the publication of this interview, the July 26 Movement will be at liberty to launch at any time revolutionary struggle as the only course to salvation."[45]

The enemy was thus alerted to the invasion plans, but the movement gained the confidence of the people, to whom it had promised that it would be fighting inside Cuba in 1956.[46]

It is important to keep in mind that when Fidel decided to take up arms once again he saw the need to establish a clear line of demarcation from other organizations and parties that also talked about using arms against Batista. The Revolutionary Directorate was not alone in coming out for armed struggle. Even sectors of the capitalist parties themselves (Authentic and Orthodox) talked about armed struggle. They brought guns into Cuba and staged armed attacks.

This explains Fidel's statements against assassinating the dictator and against hasty armed actions in the cities. A few weeks after arriving in Mexico he read in the press about the blowing up of an ammunition depot in Havana. He said: "I understand impatience at this time but I think that the time is still not ripe for the revolution. The uproar is artificial. A real explosion must be prepared with more knowledge and more care."[47]

Shortly afterward he wrote: "We oppose violent methods directed against persons from any opposition organization who hold views different from ours, and we are radically opposed to assassination. We do not practice tyrannicide. . . .

"The Cuban people want more than a simple change in command. Cuba longs for a radical change in all fields of public and social life. . . ."[48]

Tactical differences also existed between the Revolutionary Directorate and Fidel.

Although both organizations stressed insurrection and a general strike to overthrow Batista, the Directorate held that Havana should be the nerve center of the struggle. It was the home of over a million people, and it was unquestionably the most important center of the country from the economic, political, and military standpoint. However, Fidel rightly said that for these reasons it was also the enemy stronghold, where the relationship of forces favored the regime, where the underground activity of the revolutionary movement was extremely limited and risky. He therefore chose Oriente Province as the terrain for the struggle. In Oriente the regime was much weaker and the population possessed great revolutionary traditions. While the Directorate concentrated its principal cadres in Havana, where they played a very important role but at a very high price — including the death of its top leader and some of its best people — Fidel prepared to land in Oriente.

After reaching the Sierra Maestra, he would fight to concentrate the most resources in that region, where the movement's best cadres were based. Top priority would be assigned to the arming of rural guerrillas. Fidel would insist that all weapons had to be sent to the mountains, a position that met with resistance from some of the July 26 Movement's own urban cadres.

Propaganda: The Key Link During Prison and Exile

Fidel was convinced even before the Moncada attack that the Cuban people, who did not understand the roots of the exploitation that they suffered and who blamed all their problems on government corruption, would be educated politically through the revolutionary struggle itself. In pursuing certain concrete goals flowing from the people's most vital interests, the revolutionary struggle would of necessity pit the exploited masses against their exploiters in actual life.

On the twentieth anniversary of the Moncada attack, Fidel summed up the elements he took into account in mapping out his political strategy.

"Even before March 10, 1952, some of us had come to the conclusion that Cuba's problems would have to be solved in a revolutionary manner, and that power had to be seized at a given moment with the masses and with arms, and that the objective had to be socialism," he explained.

"But how could we lead the masses along that road, especially in view of the fact that most of them were not conscious of the exploitation from which they suffered and believed that government corruption was the main cause of the social ills, together with the fact that since they were subjected to a relentless anticommunist barrage, they were afraid and prejudiced and were hemmed in by the narrow horizon of bourgeois-democratic ideas?

"In our opinion, the masses, tired of the arbitrariness, abuses, and corruption of the rulers, embittered by poverty, unemployment, and destitution, although they still failed to see the road to a real solution, would nonetheless be the driving force of the revolution.

"Revolutionary struggle itself, with concrete and defined objectives, which would involve their most essential interests and would in practical life pit them against their exploiters, would politically educate them. The class struggle sparked by the advancing revolution itself would sweep away like a house of cards the prejudices and ignorance in which their oppressors kept them.

"The March 10 coup, which raised popular discontent and frustration to a high point, and especially the cowardly vacillation of the capitalist parties and their most authoritative leaders, forced our movement to take on the leadership of the struggle and created a suitable conjuncture for applying these ideas. The political strategy of the struggle launched by the July 26 Movement was based on them.

"The first revolutionary laws would be decreed as soon as the city of Santiago was in our hands, and they would be publicized in all the media. We would call on the people to fight against Batista and for the implementation of those objectives. We would call on all the workers in the country to stage a revolutionary general strike over the heads of the yellow unions and the leaders in the pay of the government. The tactic of the war would be accepted in the course of events. If the city could not be held with the thousand guns that we planned to seize from the enemy there, we would launch guerrilla struggle in the Sierra Maestra."[49]

The first attempt to overthrow Batista failed. A considerable number of Moncada fighters were killed after being captured by the enemy. Fidel and twenty-eight of his comrades were sentenced to prison terms of several years, with the exception of Haydée Santamaría and Melba Hernández, whose terms were reduced to six months.

During that time and the subsequent period of exile in Mexico, where the *Granma* expedition was organized, the work of political propaganda was the decisive link in

Fidel's strategy for preparing the political army of the revolution.

Fidel's first big effort in the harsh conditions of prison was to write down his defense speech and get it to the outside. Once he had successfully reconstructed this speech and succeeded in getting it out of the prison, he instructed Santamaría and Hernández — who had been released on February 20 — to have 100,000 copies printed. They were to be distributed throughout Cuba within four months. Copies were sent to all journalists, teachers' organizations, attorneys' offices, and other professional groups.[50]

"The document is of decisive importance," Fidel wrote. "It contains our program and our ideology, without which it is impossible to expect anything great...."[51] "It is a courageous, advanced program which is in itself an essential part of the revolutionary strategy."[52]

The leader of the July 26 Movement felt then that "propaganda was vital. Without it there can be no mass movement and without a mass movement there can be no revolution."[53]

The following day he again underscored the decisive role played by propaganda. Fidel had devoted a great deal of effort to the organization of a political movement and especially to the small detachment of Moncada fighters. But in light of the situation the movement found itself in after that setback, he held that the job of the day was not, as many might have thought in such circumstances, to "organize revolutionary cells to have a certain number of people under command."

Rather, he said, "our immediate job right now is to rally public opinion in our favor, promote our ideas, and earn the backing of the masses of the people. Our revolutionary program is the most complete, our line is the clearest, our history is the most self-sacrificing. We have the right to win the trust of the people, without which, as I have said a thousand times, there can be no revolution."

In another part of this letter he stressed that "any immediate plan for violent action" must be cast aside in order to assign at that time "absolute priority to the speech ['History Will Absolve Me']."

Before July 26, 1953, the members of the movement were "anonymous pioneers of those ideas." Now, after the abortive actions which nonetheless resounded all over Cuba, they had to "fight for them openly. . . . Our tactics must be completely new. Before we were just a handful, now we must merge with the people."[54]

While Fidel was in prison, he developed ideas for propaganda. The first was to make "History Will Absolve Me" available throughout the country. The second, closely linked to the first, was to mobilize the people to call for an amnesty for the Moncada fighters and for all political prisoners. He worked hard to break the silence with which the regime sought to surround the Moncada attack and the ensuing slaughter of a large number of prisoners without any trial whatsoever. And he succeeded.

The wide circulation of "History Will Absolve Me" beginning in October 1954 made Fidel Castro "conspirator number one, active day and night, appearing in a dozen places at once, and eluding the forces of repression that sought to follow him and stop him from raising the people's consciousness — since, of course, he was already in prison."[55]

In January 1955 the central leader of the July 26 Movement thought of a new idea. Ñico López and Calixto García — who had participated in the attack on the Bayamo garrison, escaped unharmed, and gone into exile — would return to be tried as Moncada fighters. The aim was to push for the reopening of the trial and stir things up just before Batista's inauguration on February 24. That would provide wide media coverage, thanks to the artificial climate of freedom of expression that had been built up by the regime leading to the November 1954 electoral farce. "The presentation of evidence," Fidel said, "would once again be the center of public attention — a perfect opportunity for expounding our ideas."[56]

That propaganda strategy and the methods used during his twenty months in prison helped to demolish the wall of silence around the heroes of July 26. Fidel's name began to be cheered at public rallies.[57] The amnesty campaign shook the country to such an extent that Batista was forced to release all the political prisoners. The Popular Socialist Party and the University Student Federation headed by José Antonio Echeverría contributed significantly to the amnesty campaign.

The PSP called for general elections, opposing both the deals cut by the capitalist parties and the "putschist" leanings of some groups representing the petty bourgeoisie.[58] Echeverría, on the other hand, said that after the November 1 farce it was naive to try to take power from the regime by way of the ballot box. "Only by militant national action that reaffirms the principles of the Cuban revolution, in which our homeland is already engaged," he wrote on April 17, 1955, in *Bohemia*, "will this dark period of our republican history be wiped out."[59]

Despite these differences the amnesty campaign succeeded in uniting, albeit informally, the members of the movement organized by Fidel and the Moncada sympathizers with the PSP and the Directorate, along with thousands more Cubans, in a broad front to press for release of the political prisoners and the end of the repression.

On May 15, 1955, Fidel and his comrades were released from prison. His plans for continuing the struggle inside Cuba, as we have seen, had to be modified in view of the situation. A few weeks later he had to go into exile. He left for Mexico to prepare an armed expedition aimed at toppling Batista. Fidel devoted a considerable portion of his time to the training of the group that would accompany him, but his prime consideration continued to be propaganda.

He worked on a series of manifestos to the Cuban

people. The first of these, with a press run of fifty thousand copies, would appear on August 16, 1955, the fourth anniversary of the death of Chibás, so that several thousand copies could be distributed at the cemetery. "You'll see how we break through the curtain of silence and start making way for our new strategy," he wrote on August 3.

The second manifesto criticized previous forms of struggle and put forward the "first slogans around insurrection and a general strike." So important did Fidel regard this manifesto that he recommended that 100,000 copies be printed.[60]

He was convinced at that time that the strength of his organization would "grow in direct proportion" to its propaganda effort.[61]

"The printing and distribution of our propaganda must be organized so as to keep it from faltering at any time," he wrote several days later. "I assign a decisive importance to this because the manifestos circulating clandestinely throughout the country not only keep up morale but do the work of thousands of activists. They transform every enthusiastic citizen into a militant supporter who repeats our arguments and ideas."[62]

We have to keep in mind that the movement's mass propaganda, which in itself engendered organization, had an even greater impact because of the standing the Moncada fighters already enjoyed in the eyes of the people.

Later, when Fidel and his forces reached the Sierra Maestra, the newspaper *Revolución* and later *Radio Rebelde*, transmitting from the heart of the mountains, would play a key role in providing accurate information on the results of the fighting between the olive-clad guerrillas and the regime's army, as well as in the political education of the people. *Revolución*, together with the FEU paper *Alma Mater*, was the first to report that Fidel had not been killed in the *Granma* landing. From then on, *Revolución* educated, organized, and guided the anti-Batista movement.

Finally, as Fidel had anticipated, the best propaganda for revolutionary ideas was the victory of the revolution itself and the measures it enacted benefiting the people of Cuba.

Let's see how Fidel put it, on the twentieth anniversary of the Moncada attack:

"The revolutionary laws pitted the exploiters and the exploited against each other in all areas. Big landowners, capitalists, landlords, bankers, big businessmen and bosses of all kinds, and their vast legion of flunkeys, reacted immediately against the revolutionary power. They acted in cahoots with imperialism — the privileged proprietor in Cuba of vast stretches of land, mines, sugar mills, banks, utilities, stores, factories; the lord and master of our economy — which no longer had an army in its service. Then the conspiracies began, with sabotage, press campaigns, threats from abroad. . . .

"Class consciousness developed in an incredible way. Very soon the workers, the farmers, the students, the revolutionary intellectuals *had to take up arms to defend their conquests from the imperialist enemy and his reactionary accomplices* . . . they shed their generous blood fighting the CIA and the bandits . . . they were prepared to wage war against the danger from abroad . . . they fought on the beaches at the Bay of Pigs and Playa Larga against the mercenary invaders.

"But by then the exploited classes had opened their eyes to reality. *They had finally found their own ideology, which was no longer that of the capitalists, the landlords, and the other exploiters, but the revolutionary ideology of the working class, Marxism-Leninism.* . . .

"Thus, on April 16, 1961, our working class, marching to bury their dead on the eve of the invasion with their rifles held high, proclaimed the socialist character of our revolution, and in its name they fought and shed their blood. An entire people was ready to die. A decisive leap in political consciousness had come about since July 26, 1953. No moral victory could be compared to that one in the glorious history of our revolution, because no people in the Americas had been subjected by imperialism to such an intense process of reactionary indoctrination, of destruction of a nationality and its historic values. No people had been so deformed over half a century, and here was that people standing up like a moral giant before its historic oppressors to sweep away in a few years that ideological burden and all the McCarthyite, anticommunist filth.

"In the struggle the people learned to recognize their internal and external class enemies and their genuine external and internal allies. In face of the sabotage of *La Coubre*[63] and the embargo on arms from capitalist sources when we needed them most, the criminal economic blockade decreed by the United States and the isolation decreed by the Latin American governments at the orders of Yankee imperialism, only the socialist camp, from Lenin's great homeland, extended a friendly and generous hand. From there came arms, petroleum, wheat, machinery, and raw materials. There markets developed for our boycotted products. From there, 10,000 kilometers away, ships ploughed the seas. And from there we received international solidarity and fraternal support."[64]

"Revolutionary ideas did not become the consciousness of a minority, of a group. They became the consciousness of the great masses of our people," he said in another speech.

"The camps had been defined; the enemies had declared themselves as such; the laboring masses, the *campesinos*, the student masses, the masses of the poor, the underprivileged masses of our nation, significant portions of the middle class, sections of the petty bourgeoisie, intellectual workers, made Marxist-Leninist ideas their own, made their own the struggle for the Socialist Revolution."[65]

Stages in the Formation of the Anti-Batista Bloc

From the time he began preparing the initial group that would later develop into the July 26 Movement, Fidel knew that the revolution could not be the "return to power of men who were morally and historically finished and who were fully responsible for the country's plight. Remember always that our prospects for victory are based on the certainty that the people will back the efforts of men with integrity, who will from the start formulate their revolutionary laws. Men who have deceived and betrayed the people cannot hope for such backing."[66]

Fidel was greatly concerned about the need for revolutionaries to project an image of complete honesty and dedication to defending the interests of the people, even at the risk of their own lives. This was demonstrated by the young people involved in the Moncada attack and their valiant defense before Batista's tribunals — a course that broke from all the methods used by the traditional politicians.

That was why Fidel regarded as a "serious ideological deviation" the leaning among some members of his organization, during his imprisonment on the Isle of Pines, toward making a pact with the Authentic Party.

If we did not rely on those politicians when we were preparing the Moncada attack, when the Authentic Party had millions, and we "were begging for pennies and suffering terrible hardships to purchase weapons," Fidel asked, how could we do so now, "totally disregarding those who gave their lives for their noble ideals?"[67]

In the June 18, 1954, letter to Haydée Santamaría and Melba Hernández, he elaborated on the issue of an accord with the Authentic Party leaders: "It would be folly to make a pact with them, following the road that has led so many Orthodox leaders to ruin. I am convinced that we must keep the movement independent, as we did in the most difficult moments, when no one wanted to pay any attention to us.

"I am aware of the great difficulties you face in your struggle, but do not despair. Remember that nothing can be attempted until we are out and that it is always necessary to wait for the right moment. Your mission is to prepare the way, keep the worthy men together — there can never be too many of them — and recruit all those who may be useful. Cuba is full of courageous men, but we must find them."[68]

In regard to the signers of the Montreal Pact he wrote to Melba around the same time:[69]

"We have had to fight alone before, during and after the events of the 26th. Now we represent a lofty and unblemished ideal, and we have the right to be the vanguard of the future. We musn't sell our souls for a mess of pottage. What position do these gentlemen hold now? They haven't changed, except to add a little word of praise to deceive us and then do as bad or worse to us as they did to the Orthodox Party — which they led into a dead end, disparaged, and then booted out like a no-good prostitute.

"I know it's hard to stand firm when the whole world is saying it's zero hour. I know all too well that everyone is desperate to get hold of a gun and that the only resource the Montreal group has is to cleverly make converts in return for weapons, but I've had enough of desperate men. They're always the most demanding and annoying ones before the struggle begins and then the ones least interested in fighting when the time comes. For them, revolution is nothing but a fine adventure.

"We have to realize that, rather than a real force, we are still an idea, a symbol — and a great potential force. It will be to Cuba's benefit if we can follow a line. We're ready to give up our lives for freedom. . . . Their only goal is power, while ours is a real revolution. They are leading the struggle now because they have millions of dollars. Tomorrow they will steal millions on the pretext that it's for the struggle. No agreement can be reached with them unless they first accept our program — not because it's ours, but because it means the only possible revolution — which doesn't, of course, exclude confiscating the property of all the crooks in all the administrations. That should hit pretty close to home. . . .

"It doesn't matter how few we are, for there's a long road ahead. If we can uphold our principles, they will one day become the banner of a real and possible revolution."[70]

As we have seen, in the first years after the Moncada action propaganda became the number one task. A small nucleus of cadres and extensive propaganda among the most diverse sectors of the people would be Fidel's strategy for building the vanguard of the revolution. But it must be remembered that the small nucleus of cadres had been prepared to give their lives in the Moncada attack. And once again, in the *Granma* landing, they would demonstrate their selflessness and devotion to the interests of the people and the country in bondage.

Large-scale propaganda rested on the authority of the Moncada fighters, a group of young people who had rejected all the political cliches used until then by the capitalist politicians, and who had found a form of struggle suited to waging a successful fight against the Batista dictatorship.

The unifying factor of the July 26 Movement *was not* Marxist-Leninist ideology, which had been assimilated only by its most advanced cadres. Rather *it was the fight against Batista in a new, armed form*, leading to radical transformations in the social as well as the political sphere, and the winning of true national sovereignty.

Fidel realized that in the McCarthyite, anticommunist climate existing in Cuba and in the world, declarations of Marxist-Leninist faith would have been absurd. The point was not to make declarations but to act and to show in deeds how correct his revolutionary formulations were.

He was so convinced of this that not even people as close to him as Che Guevara, who spent months with him in exile and many more in the Sierra Maestra, were aware of his deepest thinking.

For a time Che was convinced that Fidel had supported the Miami Pact, a very conservative agreement, and that Fidel was just a radical bourgeois leader.

This is what Che wrote to René Ramos Latour (Daniel), an urban leader of the July 26 Movement, in December 1957, after Fidel had come out publicly against the Miami Pact:

"I always regarded Fidel as a genuine leader of the left-wing bourgeoisie, although he himself was outstanding because of his exceptional brilliance that placed him far above his class. That was my opinion when I joined the struggle. I honestly did not think it had any hopes of going beyond the liberation of the country, and I was prepared to leave Cuba once the conditions of further struggle turned the action of the movement toward the right. What never occurred to me was the radical change made by Fidel in his statements about the Miami Pact. I regarded as impossible what I later learned — that is, that the will of the genuine leader and only driving force of the movement could be so distorted. I thought what I now feel ashamed to have thought."[71]

The letter explains part of Che's farewell message to Fidel in April 1965, before he left for the Bolivian jungle:

"Recalling my past life, I believe I have worked with sufficient honor and dedication to consolidate the revolutionary victory. My only serious failing was not having confided more in you from the first moments in the Sierra Maestra, and not having understood quickly enough your qualities as a leader and a revolutionary. I have lived magnificent days, and I felt at your side the pride of belonging to our people in the brilliant yet sad days of the Caribbean crisis."[72]

Fidel was convinced that the dispersal of forces was the "death of the revolution" while the unity of all the revolutionaries was the "death of the dictatorship."[73] However, before tackling the building of a broad civic movement, as Luis Conte Agüero proposed to him in the middle of 1954, Fidel felt that his first aim must be to "organize the members of the July 26 Movement and forge an indestructible unity among all the combatants — those in exile, those in prison and out, over eighty young people involved in the same chapter of history and sacrifice. The importance of that well-disciplined human nucleus is incalculable for the development of cadres for the organization of civic struggle and insurrection. . . .

"The task of uniting all our combatants must come first," he wrote on August 14, 1954, "because it would be a shame if the lack of basic work in motivation were to lead to serious losses in our ranks. Thanks to the experience of the period before July 26, I can assure you that a tried and trusted young person is worth a thousand others and that perhaps the most difficult and time-consuming task is to find people of quality and prepare them so that their initial participation will be decisive. Starting with the people we now have, we can greatly multiply our forces, that is, forces that are prepared to join other similar forces in disciplined fashion in order to build the necessary momentum to defeat the existing political system."

Once this initial aim was attained, the next task was the formation of a civic movement which "must have sufficient strength to win power either through peaceful or revolutionary means, otherwise it would run the risk of having it snatched away, as happened to the Orthodox Party, just two months before elections."[74]

However he was not optimistic in regard to the possibilities of building such a movement quickly. He knew that uniting such disparate personalities would be a considerable feat. He was aware that "one of the greatest obstacles to the formation of such a movement is the excess of individualism and ambition on the part of groups and leaders. The difficulty is getting each courageous man to place himself at the service of a cause, an ideology, and a discipline, free of vanity and ambition."

He thus confessed that what he most admired in Martí "is not so much his feats in battle but that huge, heroic, and silent task of uniting the Cubans for struggle." He was convinced that without such an effort "Cuba would still be a Spanish colony or a Yankee protectorate."

Among the conditions he regarded as "indispensable" for the formation of a genuine civic movement were a minimum of agreement in the ideological sphere, good discipline, and above all, a recognized leadership.

"You cannot build a movement if everyone feels he has the right to issue public statements without consulting with anyone. Nor can anything be expected of a movement that is made up of anarchistic-type individuals who at the first disagreement go off on their own tack, thereby tearing apart and destroying the movement."

A mechanism had to be created that would make it possible to "destroy completely anyone who tries to build tendencies, cliques, splits or to rise up against the movement."

Fidel also held that the movement's "program must take up fully, concretely, and courageously the country's critical economic and social problems in order to offer the masses a truly new and promising message."[75]

Once the initial nucleus of the July 26 Movement was consolidated and it had definitively broken with the Orthodox Party leadership (March 1956), he redoubled his efforts to unite the revolutionary forces.

Several months later, in September 1956, these efforts culminated in the signing, with José Antonio Echeverría, of what came to be known as the Mexico Pact. This document stated that "both organizations have decided to solidly join their efforts to overthrow the dictatorship and carry out the Cuban revolution." The signers criticized those who, after having called for free general elections, now accepted the mid-term elections proposed by the regime. Both the July 26 Movement and the Directorate felt that objective conditions existed for a revolution in Cuba and that revolutionary preparations were sufficiently advanced to be able to "offer the people their liberation in 1956."

The two organizations felt at the time that the victory against Batista would take place through "an insurrection backed up by a general strike."

The manifesto called for the unity of "all the revolutionary, moral, and civic forces of the country, the students, the workers, the youth organizations, and all worthy people of Cuba, to assist them in this struggle, which is sealed with the decision to win or to die."[76]

The Mexico Pact ideologically united the fighting young people of the July 26 Movement and the Directorate in regard to the aims of the revolution. However, the unity process had still not gone far enough to be able to map out a single military strategy. Each organization selected a different arena of struggle.[77] Despite those differences the two leaders were wise enough to reach unity agreements in the area where it was possible at that time. They granted each other the freedom to carry out the plans each regarded as best tactically, although each force had an assigned task within the general plan.

Fidel would resume armed struggle before the end of 1956, as he had promised, landing in Cuba with an armed contingent and opening a guerrilla front in the eastern mountains. The Revolutionary Directorate would simultaneously work toward an armed insurrection with its center in Havana, preceded by actions that would produce public ferment. For their part, the members of the July 26 Movement inside Cuba would stage all kinds of actions to confuse the enemy throughout the country, but chiefly in Oriente.[78] In this way the forces of the dictatorship would have to react in different parts of the country.

The process of building unity among the revolutionary forces represented by the July 26 Movement, the Revolutionary Directorate, and the Popular Socialist Party advanced slowly. It would not be completed until two years after the victory of the revolution, with the founding in 1961 of the Integrated Revolutionary Organizations (ORI).

Meanwhile Fidel had been implementing a policy of broad unity with all the anti-Batista forces.

But just when did the political strategist place a policy of broad unity in the foreground? Only when the July 26 Movement had become a decisive force on the political scene. Fidel realized that if he pushed for unity before the movement was strong enough he ran the risk of trailing after the procapitalist forces.

Pacts with Capitalist Forces

The first step toward unity with nonrevolutionary forces came on July 12, 1957, when Fidel's political authority was already well established among the people.

Among those who made their way up to the Sierra Maestra were representatives of the capitalist opposition such as Raúl Chibás, president of the Cuban People's Party (Orthodox) and brother of the late Eduardo Chibás, and Felipe Pazos, former president of the National Bank of Cuba and a close associate of Authentic Party leader Carlos Prío Socarrás. Dialogue was not easy. The revolutionary youth of the people, represented by the July 26 Movement, and the procapitalist anti-Batista forces held many disparate views.

Finally, thanks to Fidel's tactical flexibility, what became known as the Sierra Manifesto was signed. In addition to stressing that uniting their forces "is the only patriotic course of action" at that time — with Batista still in power thanks to his success in keeping his enemies divided — the signers expressed their readiness to participate in "truly free, democratic, impartial elections." For that to happen, they said, Batista would have to be replaced by "a neutral provisional government" with the support of all the opposition parties, all the civic institutions, and all the revolutionary sectors.

The proposals contained in the manifesto were:

"1. Formation of a civilian-revolutionary front with a common strategy of struggle.

"2. Immediate appointment of an individual to head the provisional government. As proof of disinterest on the part of the opposition leaders and of impartiality on the part of the appointee, the selection will be made by the civic institutions acting together.

"3. A declaration to the country that, in view of the seriousness of the situation, the only possible solution is the resignation of the dictator and the handing over of power to the person who enjoys the trust and majority support of the nation as expressed through its representative organizations.

"4. A declaration that the civilian-revolutionary front neither calls for nor accepts any kind of mediation or intervention by another nation in Cuba's internal affairs. To the contrary, it supports the denunciations of human rights violations made by Cuban emigrés before international bodies and asks the United States to suspend all arms shipments to Cuba for the duration of the present regime of terror and dictatorship.

"5. A declaration that the civilian-revolutionary front, in keeping with republican and proindependence tradition, will not accept any sort of military junta as a provisional government of the republic.

"6. A declaration that the civilian-revolutionary front plans to remove the army from politics and guarantee the nonpolitical status of the armed forces. The soldiers have nothing to fear from the Cuban people but much to fear from the corrupt clique that sends them to their death in fratricidal struggle.

"7. A formal pledge that the provisional government will hold general elections for all national, provincial, and municipal posts within one year, in keeping with the norms of the 1940 constitution and the 1943 electoral code, and will immediately turn over power to the victorious candidate.

"8. A declaration that the provisional government will act in keeping with the following program:

"A. Immediate release of all political prisoners, both civilian and military.

"B. Full guarantee of freedom of information to the news media and of all individual and political rights guaranteed by the constitution.

"C. Appointment of provisional mayors in all the municipalities after consultation with the civic institutions of the locality.

"D. Suppression of all forms of government corruption and adoption of measures designed to enhance the efficiency of all organisms of the state.

"E. Establishment of a civil service.

"F. Democratization of union politics through free elections in all union locals and industry-wide federations.

"G. Immediate launching of an all-out campaign against illiteracy and for civic education, stressing the duties and the rights of the citizen in relation to society and the fatherland.

"H. Putting in place the foundations for an agrarian reform designed to distribute unused land and transform into owners all the cane growers who rent their land and all sharecroppers, tenant farmers, and squatters who work small plots of land owned either by the state or private persons, through payment of compensation to the former owners.

"I. Adoption of a sound financial policy designed to safeguard the stability of our currency and promote the use of the nation's credit in productive projects.

"J. Acceleration of the industrialization process and creation of new jobs. . . .

"Political parties and civic institutions do not have to declare themselves insurgent and come to the Sierra Maestra in order to join this front. It is sufficient for them to refuse any kind of support for the regime's arranged elections and to declare before the country, the armed forces, and international public opinion that after five years of useless efforts, of continual deception and rivers of blood, Cuba's only solution is the resignation of Batista. . . ."[79]

There is no question that the minimal program put forward by Fidel in "History Will Absolve Me" is much more radical than that resulting from the agreement between the procapitalist representatives and the rebels in the Sierra Maestra. The latter makes no mention of workers sharing in company profits nor of the cane growers sharing in the yield of the crop. Nor does it speak of the confiscation of ill-gotten property or the nationalization of the electric and telephone companies, which, together with consistent implementation of agrarian reform, would in practice become anti-imperialist measures.

However, a close reading of the Sierra Manifesto discloses Fidel's skill in formulating the programmatic measures in which traditional politics, foreign intervention, and military coup are rejected as political solutions, and a series of tasks of a democratic nature are set forth. In practice these measures would aid at the institutional level the expression of the real popular support that the July 26 Movement had already achieved. In addition there were measures in line with the interests of the nationalist sectors of the capitalist class that would of necessity clash with imperialist economic policy.

The fundamental thing was to get rid of Batista and prevent a reformist solution of Batistaism without Batista or a foreign intervention. That, along with the adoption of truly democratic measures, would unquestionably enable the July 26 Movement to come to power.

Several weeks later, in September, this time in Miami, representatives of the capitalist class, Prío Socarrás and Pazos, using their status as signers of the Sierra Manifesto along with Fidel Castro, participated in the formation of a National Liberation Junta. This took place in the midst of a diplomatic offensive by the new United States ambassador in a bid to promote the unification of the capitalist forces against Batista and, in so doing, to isolate the revolutionary movement. The National Liberation Junta was made up of the Cuban Revolutionary Party (Authentic), the Authentic Organization, the Cuban People's Party (Orthodox), the University Student Federation (FEU), the Revolutionary Labor Directorate, the March 13 Revolutionary Directorate, the Democratic Party, and a July 26 Movement delegation that was not authorized by the leadership to take such a step.

The programmatic document that emerged from the Miami meeting differed on two key points from the Sierra Manifesto. It eliminated the explicit rejection of foreign intervention and the repudiation of the formation of a military junta to govern the country provisionally. These were both "cardinal principles" in the eyes of July 26 Movement.

On December 14 Fidel publicly declared his disagreement with the Miami Pact. He stressed that this break was not motivated by the procedure followed — that is, using the July 26 Movement without consulting its principal leaders — but rather the violation of key points of the Sierra Maestra agreement.

In a letter to the opposition organizations, Fidel wrote:

"Elimination from the unity document of the explicit declaration rejecting any foreign intervention in Cuba's internal affairs reveals a lukewarm patriotism and a most eloquent cowardice.

"Declaring that we oppose intervention means asking that there be no intervention in favor of the revolution because that would be detrimental both to our sovereignty and to a principle that concerns all the peoples of the Americas. But it also means asking that there be no intervention in favor of the dictatorship in the form of shipments of planes, bombs, tanks, and up-to-date weapons with which it remains in power — as, more than anyone, we and most especially the peasant population of the Sierra Maestra have personally experienced. In a word, achieving the end of intervention means the overthrow of the dictatorship. . . .

"The unity document eliminates the explicit declaration

of the rejection of any sort of military junta to rule the country provisionally.

"The worst that could happen to the nation at this time — because it would be accompanied by the hoax that Cuba's problem had been solved with the removal of the dictator — would be the replacement of Batista by a military junta. And some civilians of the worst kind, who even supported March 10 but have since broken with Batista — perhaps because they are even more militaristic and ambitious than he is — are thinking about such solutions. Only the enemies of the nation's progress would favor such a development.

"If experience has shown in the Americas that all military juntas once again lean toward autocracy; if the worst of the evils that have plagued this continent is the entrenchment of the military castes in countries with fewer wars than Switzerland and more generals than Prussia; if one of our people's most legitimate aspirations in this crucial hour in which their democratic, republican future will either be saved or defeated for many years is to uphold, as the most precious legacy of their liberators, the tradition of civilian government that goes back to the wars for independence and would be broken the day a uniformed junta headed the republic (not even the most glorious generals of our wars for independence ever attempted that, in war or peace); how can we give up everything out of fear of offending sensibilities (more imagined than real among honorable military men who may support us) by eliminating such an important statement of principles?

"Is it really not understood that a timely statement of principle could ward off the danger of a military junta that would serve only to continue the civil war? All right, then: we do not hesitate to declare that if a military junta replaces Batista, the July 26 Movement will proceed resolutely with its liberation campaign. It is preferable to fight more today than to fall tomorrow into new and unbreachable abysses. No military junta, no puppet government run by the military! A government of civilians with decency and honesty, the soldiers back to their barracks, and let each fulfill their duty! . . . "

"The important thing for the revolution," Fidel wrote in the same letter "is not unity in itself but the foundations on which it is based, the way in which it is implemented, and the patriotic intentions that inspire it."[80]

After seven months the civilian front had not consolidated itself, but the Rebel Army had. It had succeeded in throwing back Batista's general offensive of June and preparing for the counteroffensive.

The year 1958 had opened with harbingers of peace. Elections for president, vice-president, senators, mayors, and city councilors were slated for July. That forced the regime to restore constitutional guarantees. The political parties reorganized and press censorship was lifted.

The country thus learned of the abuses committed by the regime, the torture and the murders, at the same time that Rebel Army activities began to be reported.

For its part the Cuban Council of Bishops set up a Commission for National Harmony composed of prominent individuals and backed by the most well-known sugarmill owners, merchants, and bankers.

"The commission sought to reach a settlement between Fidel and Batista under which the Rebel Army would lay down its arms, political prisoners would be released, exiles would be allowed to return, and free elections would be held with the participation of the July 26 Movement as just another traditional political party. The peace effort was clearly a maneuver completely at the service of the regime. In an open letter of March 9, 1958, Commander Fidel Castro denounced the goals of the commission, thereby putting an end to its brief life."[81]

One month later, on April 9, the general strike was a failure. Then, in June, Batista, emboldened by events, launched a large-scale offensive aimed at wiping out the Rebel Army. It met with complete failure. The enemy emerged severely weakened while the revolutionary movement had been greatly strengthened by brilliant military successes against large forces.

That was the situation on July 20, 1958, when Fidel judged that the time had come to call for the formation of a broad civilian-revolutionary front. Representatives of a very broad spectrum of political and social forces signed a unity document that became known as the Caracas Pact.[82]

First, this very important manifesto described the situation in Cuba at the time:

"Rebellion has spread throughout the country. In the mountainous regions of Cuba new battle fronts have been formed, and on the plains, guerrilla columns relentlessly harass the enemy. Right now, in the Sierra Maestra, thousands upon thousands of soldiers, in the biggest offensive Batista has ever attempted, are being thrown back by the courage of the revolutionary fighters who defend Cuba's free territory inch by inch, down to their last drop of blood.

"In Oriente, forces of Column Number Six, called *Frank País*,[83] control a third of the province and are waging big battles. On the Oriente plains, Column Number Two is fighting from Manzanillo to Nuevitas in Camagüey. In Las Villas, the Escambray front of the Revolutionary Directorate has been fighting bravely for several months, staging incursions in other parts of Cuba's central province. Also fighting in that province are groups of Authentics and of the July 26 Movement. In Cienfeugos and Yaguajay, revolutionary guerrilla units fight and move with intensity. Small guerrilla units are operating in Matanzas and Pinar del Río. In every corner of Cuba a fight to the death is being waged between freedom and tyranny, while outside the country large numbers of exiles and emigrés strive to free their oppressed homeland."

Second, the Caracas Pact called for the formation of a broad national front against Batista, without the exclusion of any sector.

"The coordination of human efforts, military resources, and civilian forces of the political and revolutionary sectors of *all the opposition groups* — civilian, military, workers, students, professionals, economic and people's organizations — can overthrow the dictatorship in a supreme effort. Therefore, the signers of this document unite our resources with the adoption of this agreement in favor of a *great civilian, revolutionary front of struggle of every sector.* Each force, standing shoulder to shoulder, contributes its patriotism and its efforts. United, let us oust from power the criminal dictatorship of Fulgencio Batista and return to Cuba the peace it yearns for and the democratic course that will lead our people toward the development of their freedom, wealth, and progress. We are all agreed on the need to unite, and this is what the people demand."

Third, the pact spoke of one of the pillars of the unity of the opposition forces, the road to eliminating the dictatorship:

"A common strategy of struggle to topple the dictatorship through *armed insurrection,* strengthening all the fighting fronts as soon as possible, arming the thousands of Cubans who are ready to fight for freedom. *Popular mobilization* of all the labor, civic, professional, and economic forces to cap the civilian effort with a *general strike,* and the military effort with *an armed action coordinated throughout the country.* This bold course will free Cuba and prevent further painful bloodshed among our best human reserves. Victory will be ours in any case, but will be delayed if our activities are not coordinated."

Fourth, the Caracas Pact presented the kind of government to be established after the fall of the dictator: a brief "provisional government" to lead the country along "constitutional and democratic channels."

Fifth, it set forth *very briefly* the main points of a minimum government program. The new government must guarantee "the punishment of the guilty, the rights of the workers, order, peace, freedom, fulfillment of international commitments, and the economic, social, and institutional progress of the Cuban people."

Sixth, it affirmed the decision to defend *"national sovereignty"* and called on the United States government to "end all military and other types of aid to the dictator."

Finally, it appealed to all social sectors to unite in the fight against Batista:

"We say to the members of the military that the time has come to deny support to the despotic regime. We have faith in them, we know that there are decent men in the armed forces. If in the past hundreds of officers and enlisted men have paid with their lives, imprisonment, exile, or retirement from active duty because of their love of freedom and their opposition to the dictatorship, there must be many others who feel the same way. This is not a war against the armed forces of the republic, but against Batista — the only obstacle to that peace desired and needed by all Cubans, civilian and military.

"We urge workers, students, professionals, businessmen and industrialists, cane growers, mill owners and farmers, and Cubans of all religions, ideologies, and races: join this fight for freedom that will overthrow the infamous tyranny that for years has soaked our soil with blood, killing off its best human resources, ruining its economy, undermining the very foundations of all Cuba's institutions, blocking the democratic, constitutional process in the country. The result has been this bloody civil war, which will end with the victory of the revolution through the united efforts of all.

"The time has come when the intelligence, patriotism, valor, and civic virtues of Cuba's men and women — especially those of us who feel deeply about our nation's historic destiny, its right to be free and become part of the democratic community — will save the oppressed homeland. Our future is great because of our history as well as Cuba's natural resources and the undeniable capacity of its sons and daughters."

The document concluded by urging "all the revolutionary, civic, and political forces" to sign the declaration. It also called for a meeting of representatives of all sectors "with no exclusions of any kind to discuss and adopt the bases of unity."[84]

The broad political front was never *formally* organized. The only organizational responses came from the Popular Socialist Party and from the Revolutionary Directorate, with which a formal unity process had been underway since 1955. Nonetheless, Batista was in fact overthrown by the joint action of all those forces.

To achieve that objective, Fidel Castro had no difficulty agreeing that the new government resulting from the revolution would be made up of prominent figures, the majority of whom were members of the big capitalist class, and that it would be a "conservative government team," as he himself would describe it later.

That proved to be of little importance because it was the Rebel Army that had defeated Batista's military forces and forced him to flee into exile. Thus one of the most important parts of the repressive apparatus of the capitalist state had been smashed.

While the government, in its big majority, was in reactionary hands, "the force of the masses and the force of arms," said Fidel, was "in revolutionary hands." This force was the real power of the revolution.

Fidel believed it was correct to have adopted that course in the first months after victory. "The existing relationship of social, political, and ideological forces . . . especially the relationship of ideological forces that still existed in the country" meant that such a government was the most suitable. The main thing, he stressed, was that the revolutionaries enjoyed the "support of the masses" and had the "Rebel Army."[85]

Conclusions

The immediate enemy and the breadth of the political front

Fidel's strategy for forging the bloc of social forces that made possible the overthrow of Batista and then the march toward socialism provides us with important lessons.

Although he was well aware that the only consistently revolutionary forces were those that were part of "the people," as he defined it, he also realized that the ruling classes had very powerful means for maintaining the status quo, including the support of the world's most powerful imperialist country.

His great historic merit lies in having known how to identify clearly the decisive link that would make it possible to seize the entire chain and enable the revolution to advance. That decisive link was the struggle against Batista.

The maximum social forces had to be united to overthrow the dictatorship. That meant uniting not only the revolutionary classes and sectors, but also the reformist sectors and even those reactionary sectors that had even the slightest contradiction with Batista.

And so, the Moncada program put forward only measures of a "bourgeois democratic" type. Although it proposed steps that would hurt United States interests, it contained no formal anti-imperialist declaration. Then, in the Sierra Pact, as we have seen, even the measures related to nationalization were eliminated. Finally the Caracas Pact, with its minimum program, contained only the most essential measures: punishment of the guilty, defense of the rights of the workers, order, peace, freedom, fulfillment of international commitments, and the quest for the economic, social, and institutional progress of the Cuban people.

Where Fidel never gave ground was on the fundamental issues, the only ones that could have stopped the development of the revolutionary process. These were: the rejection of foreign military interference, repudiation of any military coup, and refusal to be part of any bloc that would exclude any force representing a sector of the people.

The most general guidelines on the need for building a broad anti-imperialist, antioligarchic front were set forth in the Second Declaration of Havana of February 4, 1962.[86] Ten years later, concerned about the lack of unity of Chile's democratic and progressive forces and concretely the absence of common views within Popular Unity (the political front that supported Salvador Allende) at a time when the advent of fascism already loomed on the horizon, Fidel repeated those words. The occasion was his December 2, 1971, farewell speech, after a visit of several weeks to Chile.

"Imperialism, making use of the great motion picture monopolies, the wire services, its reactionary magazines, books, and newspapers, uses the most subtle lies to promote division and to inculcate the ignorant with a fear of and a superstition about revolutionary ideas, ideas which should bring fear only to the powerful exploiters and their traditional privileges.

"Divisionism, a product of all kinds of prejudice, false ideas and lies; sectarianism; dogmatism; the lack of general concepts in the analysis of the role of each social stratum, with its parties, organizations and leaders; all these obstruct the necessary unity of action which should exist among the democratic and progressive forces of our people. These are the weaknesses of growth, childhood ailments of the revolutionary movement, which should become a thing of the past. It is possible to organize the immense majority of the people in the anti-imperialist and antifeudal struggle for the goals of liberation which unite the efforts of the working class, the peasants, the intellectual workers, the petty bourgeoisie and the most progressive sectors of the national bourgeoisie. Together, these sectors constitute the immense majority of the population, great social forces which are capable of doing away with imperialist domination and feudal oligarchy. From the old militant Marxist to the sincere Catholic who has nothing to do with the Yankee monopolies and the feudal landowners, all can and must fight side by side in this broad movement for the welfare of their nations, for the welfare of their people, and for the welfare of America.

"This movement can also include the progressive elements in the armed forces, which have also been humiliated by the Yankee military missions, by the acts of treason perpetrated against the national interests by the feudal oligarchies and by the sacrifice of the national sovereignty to the dictates of Washington.

"These ideas were expressed ten years ago and do not vary one iota from the ideas we hold today."[87]

But that broad policy of alliances that Fidel had in mind from the beginning — which included special concern for winning over the greatest possible number of members of the repressive apparatus of the state (remember the words he addressed to the military and to the judges in "History Will Absolve Me") — was implemented in keeping with certain strategic considerations.

Fidel first sought unity with the revolutionary forces, and only after efforts in that direction did he call for broader unity. It is important to note that failure to achieve full unity among the revolutionaries did not prevent him from moving toward broader unity. However, he took concrete steps in that regard only when the July 26 Movement had become a considerable force and its strategy for struggle had been successfully tested in practice — when it had decisive weight on the political scene. Otherwise, as we've pointed out before, the movement would have run the risk of trailing after the capitalist forces.

Reflecting, in December 1961, on the process of unity with the capitalist forces and concretely on the repudiation of the Miami Pact, he said:

"We were left on our own, but at that moment it was a thousand times better to stand alone than in bad company. . . ."

"Why is it that back when there were just 120 of us in arms, we weren't interested in broad unity with all the organizations in exile, while later, when we numbered in the thousands, we were interested in that broad unity? The answer is simple: when there were just 120 of us, unity would have meant a clear-cut majority for conservative and reactionary elements or representatives of interests that were not revolutionary, even though they opposed Batista. We would have been a tiny force in such a union. However, toward the end of the struggle, when all those organizations were convinced that the movement was headed to victory and that the tyranny was going to be defeated, then they became interested in unity. And we were by then a decisive force within it."[88]

The unity of the revolutionary forces

Fidel provided some extremely interesting views on the formation of the unity of the revolutionary forces in a talk with Chilean students in 1971:

"The ideal thing in politics is unity of opinion, unity of doctrine, unity of forces and unity of command, as in a war. A revolution is just like a war. It is difficult to imagine a battle, being in the midst of a battle, with ten different military strategies and ten different sets of tactics. The ideal thing is unity. That is the ideal, but reality is something else. I believe that every country must get used to waging its battles in whatever conditions it finds itself. Let's say it's impossible to attain total unity. Well let's get some unity on this opinion, on this idea and on that other idea. We must seek unity on objectives, unity on specific questions. If it's impossible to achieve the ideal of absolute unity, let's get together on a number of objectives.

"A single command — or if you wish, a single general staff — is the ideal thing, but it isn't always possible. Therefore, we must get used to making do with what we have, with reality."[89]

The Cuban experience provides three important lessons in relation to the process of unification of the revolutionary forces:

First, as Fidel put it, the revolutionary leaders must have as a central concern advancing the process of unity of the revolutionary forces, and to do so they must use minimum, not maximum, objectives as the point of departure. An example of this is the Mexico Pact between the July 26 Movement and the Revolutionary Directorate.

Second, what aids the unification of the revolutionary forces most is the implementation of a strategy that will prove to be the most correct one in the struggle against the main enemy. If the results are satisfactory, the other truly revolutionary forces will join during the struggle, at the moment of victory, or in the months or years to follow.

If unity at all levels is sought too early, before conditions are ripe for it, what you might get is a purely formal sort of unity that could fall apart as soon as it runs into difficulties. Or, a minority with a correct strategy could give it up in order to submit to the majority view, with negative consequences for the revolutionary process as a whole.

Third, all the participants must have equal rights and any "superiority complex" that might crop up in one or another of the organizations must be fought. This is very important for achieving lasting unity of the revolutionary forces, and — something that Fidel always urged strongly — for a correct evaluation of the contribution of each of the revolutionary forces, without establishing shares of power either in terms of their degree of participation in the victory of the revolution or on the basis of the number of members of each organization.

Fidel's most valuable contributions on this issue came about in the course of his fight against sectarianism, especially in what became known as the first Escalante trial, in March 1962. Aníbal Escalante was organization secretary of the ORI (Integrated Revolutionary Organizations) — the first effort to institutionalize the unity of the revolutionary forces after the victory of the revolution. He set out to take over all posts and duties with "old Marxist militants," which in Cuba meant the members of the Popular Socialist Party, the only Marxist party existing before the revolution.

Instead of a free organization of revolutionaries, what was being created was a "yoke," a "straitjacket," an "army of tamed and submissive revolutionaries," Fidel said. He stressed then that it was necessary to fight both the sectarianism "of the Sierra Maestra" and the sectarianism "of the old Marxist party members."

In this regard he said:

"The revolution is superior to what each of us may have done. It is superior and it is more important than each of the organizations that were here: the 26th [of July Movement], the Partido Socialista Popular, the Directorio — than all of them. The revolution by itself is much more important than all that.

"What is the revolution? It is a great trunk which has its roots. Those roots, coming from different directions, were united in the trunk. The trunk begins to grow. The roots are important, but what begins to grow is the trunk of a great tree, of a very tall tree, whose roots came together and were joined in the trunk. All of us together made the trunk. The growing of the trunk is all that remains for us to foster and together we will continue to make it grow. . . .

"What matters is not what each of us has done separately, *compañeros*, the important thing is what we are going to do together, what we have been doing together for a long time now. And what we are doing together is of interest to all of us equally, *compañeros*."[90]

On the same day he gave another speech, referring to his personal experience: "I, too, belonged to an organization. But the glories of that organization are the glories of Cuba, they are the glories of the people, they belong to all of us. And there came a day that I stopped belonging to that organization. Which day? The day when we had made a revolution greater than our organization, the day we had a people with us, a movement far greater than our organization, near the end of the war, when we already had a victorious army that would become the army of the revolution and of all the people, at the time of the victory, when the entire people joined us and demonstrated their support, their sympathy, their strength.

"And as we moved through towns and cities, I saw lots of men and women, hundreds and thousands of men and women with the red and black uniforms of the July 26 Movement. But many more thousands wore uniforms that weren't black and red but were the workshirts of workers and farmers and other men and women of the people. And since that day, honestly, in my heart, I left the movement that we loved, under whose banners we had fought, and I joined the people. I belonged to the people, to the revolution, because we had truly accomplished something that was greater than ourselves."[91]

Notes

1. Fidel Castro, "La estrategia del Moncada" (The Moncada strategy), a 1973 interview with Swedish reporters, *Cuba Internacional* 100 (January 1978). Reprinted in *Casa de las Americas* 109 (July-August 1978).

2. Eduardo ("Eddie") Renato Chibás y Rivas was a member of the 1927 University Student Directorate (DEU) together with Antonio Guiteras and others. He launched the fight against Gerardo Machado's unconstitutional second term as president. He fought the Machado tyranny and that of Mendieta-Caffery-Batista in the thirties. He was a delegate to the 1940 constitutional convention and later a member of the House of Representatives and the Senate as a member of the Cuban Revolutionary Party, known as the Authentic Party. He subsequently left the Authentics and in 1947 founded the Cuban People's Party (Orthodox). By the time of the 1948 elections, it had become a powerful political force. (Mario Mencía, *Time Was on Our Side* [Havana: Editora Política, 1982], p. 110).

3. "The small group that worked on the organization of the movement was made up of people with very advanced ideas. We had Marxist study programs; our leadership group studied Marxism throughout that period. In fact, we could say that the organization's central leaders were already Marxists. . . . Back in my university days, my contact with Marxist ideas led me to acquire a revolutionary outlook. From then on my entire political strategy was worked out within a Marxist framework." (Castro, "La estrategia," p. 8).

José Martí — essayist, poet, and revolutionary leader — founded the Cuban Revolutionary Party and initiated the second Cuban war of independence in 1895; he was killed the same year. Martí is a national hero in Cuba.

4. Carlos Manuel de Céspedes was the central leader of the first war of independence, which began in 1868; he was killed in the fighting. Ignacio Agramonte and Máximo Gómez were also leaders of that war. Antonio Maceo was an outstanding general in both the first and second wars of independence.

5. Fidel Castro, July 26, 1973, speech, in *Historia de la revolución cubana (Selección de discursos sobre temas historicos)* (History of the Cuban revolution [selection of speeches on historical themes]) (Havana: Editora Política, 1980), pp. 267-69).

6. On August 5, 1951, during his Sunday evening radio broadcast, Chibás delivered an address that became known as "The Final Call." His closing words were: "Fellow members of the Orthodox Party, forward! For economic independence, political freedom, and social justice! Sweep the thieves from government office! People of Cuba, arise and move! Awake, Cuban people! This is my final call!" After these words, he took his pistol and shot himself in the stomach. On August 16, less than a year before the scheduled presidential elections in which many thought he would be the victor, Eduardo Chibás died in Havana, after eleven days of agony. (Mencía, *Time Was on Our Side*, p. 110).

7. Castro, "La estrategia," p. 8.

8. Castro, "La estrategia," p. 10.

9. Castro, "La estrategia," p. 8.

10. On March 10, 1952, Gen. Fulgencio Batista staged a coup d'etat to prevent an Orthodox Party victory in the elections slated for June. Batista suspended the 1940 constitution.

11. Castro, "La estrategia," p. 10.

12. Mario Mencía, "La concepción del asalto al Moncada" (The conception of the Moncada attack), *Bohemia* (July 20, 1984), p. 87.

13. Fidel Castro, December 1, 1961, television appearance, in *Obra Revolucionaria* 46 (December 2, 1961), p. 16. Reprinted in *La revolución cubana, 1953-1962* (The Cuban revolution) (Mexico City: Era, 1972), pp. 388-89.

14. Raúl Castro, "VIII aniversario del 26 de julio" (Eighth anniversary of July 26), in *Selección de lecturas de Cuba* (Selection of readings on Cuba) (Havana: Editora Política, 1984), vol. 2, pp. 151-64.

15. Castro, *La revolución cubana*, p. 388.

16. Ibid.

17. Fidel Castro, December 12, 1953, letter to Luis Conte Agüero, in *Cartas del presidio (anticipo de una biografía de Fidel Castro)* (Letters from prison: anticipation of a biography of Fidel Castro) (Havana: Editorial Lex, 1959), p. 20-21.

Luis Conte Agüero was a young and well-regarded journalist who belonged to the Orthodox Party. Fidel, while in prison, thought highly of him because of his courageous defense of the political prisoners. Conte Agüero served as a kind of liaison between the Cuban leader and the news media. However, after the 1959 revolutionary victory, Conte Agüero's extreme egotism and opportunism — evident when one reads his selection of letters for publication, in which Fidel highly praised him — led him into openly counterrevolutionary positions. He finally left the country.

18. Castro, *La revolución cubana*, p. 87.

19. This statement, signed by Fidel, appeared in the Cuban magazine *Bohemia*, April 1, 1956.

20. Castro, *La revolución cubana*, pp. 91, 92. An English-language translation appears in Jules Dubois, *Fidel Castro* (New York: Bobbs-Merrill, 1959), pp. 123-24.

21. Castro, *La revolución cubana*, p. 388.

22. Castro, *La revolución cubana*, p. 390.

23. Seven years later, PSP General Secretary Blas Roca would make an important correction of that view at the Eighth National Assembly of the party, in August 1960. Roca said that the Moncada attack "was not conceived as a classic putsch, notwithstanding the forms it adopted. The intention behind the attack was not to seize the government but to launch a revolution.

"That was why the target was not Fort Columbia . . . or some other Havana fortress but rather a garrison loaded with guns way at the end of the island. Its capture would have made it possible to arm the people and build a center of revolutionary struggle."

This assessment appears to have sparked discussion. In his final speech to the meeting, Roca found it necessary to say that while in 1953 Moncada had not seemed to be the "most suitable course," as time went by history had developed and "the results of the action were clearly visible.

"When an event occurs you may hold any opinion you like, you may say it is good or bad, but your opinion is confirmed or negated by history, by the unfolding of events. When doctors prescribe drugs, they assume the medicine will do the patient good, but they must wait. Sometimes the medicine kills the patient, and doctors become convinced that it was not good for the illness, and the patient never finds out. But if the medicine works, then everything is fine and the prediction is confirmed." Because of that, he said, "When years have gone by, when history has unfolded, it is possible to determine the results of that action," and the assembly can adopt a position on the event. (*VIII Asamblea Nacional del Partido Socialista Popular* [Eighth national assembly of the Popular Socialist Party] [Havana: Ediciones Populares, 1960], pp. 67, 405, 406).

24. On objective conditions and the conditions of structural crisis, *see* "Revolución y situación revolucionaria" (Revolution and the revolutionary situation), in Harnecker, *La revolución social*.

25. Castro, *La revolución cubana*, pp. 389-91.

26. *Anuario estadístico de Cuba 1958: Censo de la industria azucarera de Cuba* (1958 Cuba statistical yearbook: Cuban sugar industry census) (Havana: Cuba economica y financiera, 1958).

27. On the role of the capitalist class in the Cuban revolution, *see* Marcos Winocur, *Las clases olvidadas en la revolución cubana* (The forgotten classes of the Cuban revolution) (Barcelona: Editorial Crítica, 1979).

28. Ramiro Abreu, *El último año de aquella república* (The final year of that republic) (Havana: Editorial Ciencias Sociales, 1984), p. 265.

29. Fidel Castro, April 9, 1968, speech, *Granma* (April 10, 1968).

30. Castro, *La revolución cubana*, pp. 438-39. On this issue *see* "Caracter proletaria y socialista de la revolución cubana" (Working class and socialist character of the Cuban revolution), in Harnecker, *La revolución social*.

31. Castro, *La revolución cubana*, p. 405.

32. Castro, *La revolución cubana*, p. 401.

33. José Antonio Echeverría was an outstanding student leader in high school. In the university, where he studied architecture, he became an active member of the University Student Federation (FEU) and took his place in the front line of the struggle against Batista. When he learned of the July 26, 1953, attack on Moncada, he expressed regret at not having been invited

to take part in that heroic action. He was elected president of the FEU and promoted the campaign for an amnesty for the political prisoners. At the end of 1955 he organized the Revolutionary Directorate. This political organization, along with the FEU, backed the big sugar strike of December 1955. Together with Fidel, he signed the September 1956 Mexico Pact, the first big step in the unity of the revolutionary forces against the dictatorship. He was killed fighting the police near Havana University after appealing to the people over the radio as part of the attack on the Presidential Palace on March 13, 1957.

34. After the trial, Fidel reconstructed and edited this speech for publication. Known to the world under the title of its final words, "History Will Absolve Me," it is reprinted as the appendix to the present volume.

35. See appendix, p. 101.

36. Castro, *La revolución cubana*, p. 404.

37. Fidel Castro, *Second Declaration of Havana* (New York: Pathfinder Press, 1962), p. 20.

38. See appendix, p. 102-3.

39. Fidel Castro, March 19, 1955, letter to Luis Conte Agüero, in Mencía, *Time Was on Our Side*, pp. 211-18. It is also quoted in Dubois, *Fidel Castro*, pp. 90-91.

40. Fidel Castro, May 15, 1955, news conference at the Isle of Pines hotel. November 1 refers to Batista's fraudulent elections in November 1954.

41. Castro, "La estrategia," p. 20.

42. *See* Mario Mencía, "La tirania descabezada a los pies" (The leaderless tyranny on its knees), *Bohemia* (July 23, 1976), p. 61.

43. Manifesto No. 1 from the July 26 Movement to the people of Cuba.

44. Fidel Castro, August 10, 1955, Message to the Congress of Orthodox Activists, OHA.

45. *Alerta* (November 19, 1956).

46. At a meeting of Cuban exiles and emigrés in New York at Palm Garden on October 30, 1955, Fidel Castro for the first time used the slogan "in 1956 we will be free or we will be martyrs." The sentence was quoted in a piece by Vicente Cubillas, Jr., then *Bohemia* correspondent in New York ("Mitin oposicionista en Nueva York," *Bohemia* [November 6, 1955]). This slogan later became popular among masses.

47. Fidel Castro, August 2, 1955, letter addressed to "Dear Sisters," a term used to conceal the identity of his comrades in the national leadership of the July 26 Movement inside Cuba.

48. Fidel Castro, October 30, 1955, letter to Vicente Cubillas, OHA.

49. Castro, July 26, 1973, speech, in *Historia*, p. 271.

50. Fidel Castro, June 18, 1954, letter to Haydée Santamaría and Melba Hernández, in Mencía, *Time Was on Our Side*, p. 125.

51. Mencía, *Time Was on Our Side*, p. 125.

52. Fidel Castro, December 12, 1953, letter to Luis Conte Agüero, in *Cartas del presidio*, p. 21.

53. Fidel Castro, June 18, 1954, letter to Melba Hernández and Haydée Santamaría, OHA.

54. Ibid.

55. Mencía, *Time Was on Our Side*, p. 182.

56. Mencía, *Time Was on Our Side*, p. 190.

57. At a rally to wind up the campaign of opposition candidate Ramón Grau San Martín, the people interrupted the speakers by insistently chanting Fidel Castro's name.

58. A. Díaz, "Examen de algunas cuestiones de la situación actual" (Examination of some issues of the current situation). Report adopted by the expanded meeting of the Executive Bureau of the National Committee of the PSP in May 1955.

59. Mencía, *Time Was on Our Side*, p. 225.

60. Fidel Castro, August 2, 1955, letter "A los compañeros de la Dirección" (To the leadership comrades), OHA.

61. Fidel Castro, August 10, 1955, letter to Melba Hernández.

62. Fidel Castro, August 29, 1955, letter to Melba Hernández.

63. *La Coubre*, a French merchant ship carrying ammunition from Belgium, was blown up in Havana harbor, March 4, 1960, killing 100 people.

64. Castro, July 26, 1973, speech, in *Historia*, pp. 274-75. Emphasis added.

65. Fidel Castro, March 26, 1962, speech "Against Bureaucracy and Sectarianism," in *Selected Speeches of Fidel Castro* (New York: Pathfinder Press, 1979), p. 52.

66. Castro, June 18, 1954, letter to Hernández and Santamaría.

67. Fidel Castro, June 19, 1954, letter to Melba Hernández and Haydée Santamaría, in Mencía, *Time Was on Our Side*, p. 158.

68. Mencía, *Time Was On Our Side*, p. 157-58.

69. The Montreal Pact was signed by Carlos Prío Socarrás of the Authentic Party and by Emilio Ochoa of the Orthodox Party. Mario Mencía writes: "The Pact, which was signed in the winter of 1952-53, consisted of two agreements: a public one, which stated the need for unity in the struggle against Batista, and a secret one, in which Prío agreed to provide the funds for the struggle. It hinged on getting support from military men within the tyrannical regime and obtaining the backing of the United States." (Mencía, *Time Was on Our Side*, p. 37)

70. Fidel Castro, May 12, 1954, letter to Melba Hernández, in Mencía, *Time Was on Our Side*, pp. 89-90.

71. Che Guevara, December 1957 letter to René Ramos Latour, a copy of the original is in the OHA.

72. Che Guevara, "Farewell Letter to Fidel," in *Che Guevara Speaks* (New York: Pathfinder Press, 1967), p. 140.

73. Fidel Castro, "Basta ya de mentiras" (Stop the lies), July 9, 1956, *Bohemia* (July 16, 1956).

74. Batista had carried out the March 10, 1952, military coup two months before scheduled elections. The polls showed the Orthodox Party would be the sure winner.

75. Fidel Castro, August 14, 1954, letter to Luis Conte Agüero, in *Cartas del presidio*, pp. 60-61.

76. Mario Mencía, "La carta de México" (The Mexico charter), *Bohemia* (September 24, 1976), pp. 87, 88.

77. Remember that an uprising in Havana was the linchpin of the Directorate's strategy.

78. Mencía, "La carta de México," p. 91.

79. Castro, *La revolución cubana*, pp. 102-3. An English-language translation appears in Dubois, *Fidel Castro*, pp. 169-71.

80. Castro, *La revolución cubana*, pp. 108-10.

81. Abreu, *El último año*, p. 100.

82. The signers included Fidel Castro, July 26 Movement; Carlos Prío Socarrás, Authentic Organization; E. Rodríguez Loeches, Revolutionary Directorate; David Salvador, Orlando Blanco, Pascasio Lineras, Lauro Blanco, José M. Aguilera, and Ángel Cofiño, Labor Unity; Manuel A. de Varona, Cuban Revolutionary Party, Authentic; Lincoln Rondón, Democratic Party; José Puente and Omar Fernández, University Student Federation; Captain Gabino Rodríguez Villaverde, former Army officer; Justo Carrillo Hernández, Montecristi Group; Ángel María San-

tos Buch, Civic Resistance Movement; and Dr. José Miró Cardona, coordinating secretary general.

83. Frank País was a central leader of the July 26 Movement and the central organizer of the movement's urban underground in Santiago de Cuba and throughout Oriente province; he was assassinated in 1957 at age 23.

84. Castro, *La revolución cubana*, pp. 123-25 (emphasis added). An English-language translation appears in Dubois, *Fidel Castro*, p. 280-82.

85. Fidel Castro, December 1, 1961, television appearance, in *La revolución cubana*, pp. 408, 410.

86. *See* Castro, *The Second Declaration of Havana*.

87. Fidel Castro, "Farewell Rally," in *Fidel Castro on Chile* (New York: Pathfinder Press, 1982), pp. 102-3.

88. Castro, *La revolución cubana*, p. 407.

89. Fidel Castro, "University of Concepción," in *Fidel Castro on Chile*, p. 45.

90. Castro, "Against Bureaucracy and Sectarianism," in *Selected Speeches*, pp. 73-74.

91. Fidel Castro, March 26, 1962, speech, in *La revolución cubana*, pp. 545-46.

Appendix:
History Will
Absolve Me

by Fidel Castro

"History Will Absolve Me" is Fidel Castro's reconstruction of his October 16, 1953, courtroom speech in his own defense against charges arising from the attack he led on the Moncada garrison on July 26 of that year. It became a basic programmatic statement of the July 26 Movement.

In bits and pieces, the speech was smuggled out of prison in the spring of 1954. In order to outfox prison censors, some of the text was hidden in matchboxes with false bottoms. Much of it was written between the lines of other letters with lemon juice, invisible until treated with heat.

While Castro had urged in a June 18, 1954, letter that "at least 100,000 copies should be distributed within four months," the movement's severe financial limitations made this impossible. According to Mario Mencía, in his book Time Was on Our Side, nearly 2,000 pesos were collected through the device of holding a raffle and selling tickets for one peso each, "but there weren't any prizes this time, for the money was to be used in the drive against the tyranny." This was enough for only 27,500 copies.

The printing was done at great risk. A commercial print shop had to be found where the work could be done clandestinely. The police were eventually tipped off about the printer, but by then, October 1954, the copies had already been shipped, and the only evidence remaining was a proof of the title page. Numerous subsequent printings made "History Will Absolve Me" available throughout Cuba and among Cubans in exile from the Batista dictatorship.

Since the victory of the Cuban revolution, it has been published in a number of languages. The present translation is based on the English-language edition published in Cuba.

1

Honorable Judges:

Never has a lawyer had to practice his profession under such difficult conditions; never has such a number of overwhelming irregularities been committed against an accused man. In this case, counsel and defendant are one and the same. As attorney he has not even been able to take a look at the indictment. As accused, for the past seventy-six days he has been locked away in solitary confinement, held totally and absolutely incommunicado, in violation of every human and legal right.

He who speaks to you hates vanity with all his being, nor are his temperament or frame of mind inclined towards courtroom poses or sensationalism of any kind. If I have had to assume my own defense before this court it is for two reasons. First, because I have been denied legal aid almost entirely, and second, only one who has been so deeply wounded, who has seen his country so forsaken and its justice so trampled on, can speak at a moment like this with words that are the blood of the heart and the essence of truth.

There was no lack of generous comrades who wished to defend me, and the Havana Bar Association appointed a courageous and competent jurist, Dr. Jorge Pagliery, dean of the bar in this city, to represent me in this case. However, he was not permitted to carry out his task. As often as he tried to see me, the prison gates were closed before him. Only after a month and a half, and through the intervention of the court, was he finally granted a ten-minute interview with me in the presence of a sergeant from the Military Intelligence Agency. Supposedly a lawyer has the right to speak with a defendant in private — and this right is respected throughout the world except in the case of a Cuban prisoner of war in the hands of an implacable tyranny that abides by no code of law, be it legal or humane. Neither Dr. Pagliery nor I were willing to tolerate such dirty spying upon our means of defense for the oral trial. Did they want to know, perhaps, beforehand, the methods we would use to reduce to dust the incredible fabric of lies they had woven around the Moncada garrison events and how we were going to expose the terrible truths they wanted to conceal at all costs? It was then that we decided that, taking advantage of my professional rights as a lawyer, I would assume my own defense.

This decision, overheard by the sergeant and reported by him to his superior, provoked a real panic. It looked like some mocking little imp was telling them that I was going to ruin all their plans. You know very well, Honorable Judges, how much pressure has been brought to bear on me in order to strip me as well of this right that is ratified by long Cuban tradition. The court could not give in to such machination, for that would have left the accused in a state of total indefensiveness. The accused, who is now exercising this right to plead his own case, will under no circumstances refrain from saying what he must say. I consider it essential that I explain, at the outset, the reason for the terrible isolation in which I have been kept; what the purpose was of keeping me silent; what was behind the plots to kill me, plots which the court is familiar with; what grave events are being hidden from the people; and the truth behind all the strange things which have taken place during this trial. I propose to do all this with utmost clarity.

2

You have publicly called this case the most significant in the history of the republic. If you sincerely believed this, you should not have allowed your authority to be stained and degraded. The first court session was September 21. Seated in the prisoner's dock, among one hundred machine guns and bayonets that had scandalously invaded the hall of justice, were more than a hundred people. The great majority had nothing to do with what had happened. They had been under preventive arrest for many days, suffering all kinds of insults and abuses in the chambers of the repressive units. But the rest of the accused, the minority, were brave and determined, ready to proudly confirm their part in the battle for freedom, ready to offer an example of unprecedented self-sacrifice and to wrench from the jail's claws those who in deliberate bad faith had been included in the trial. Those who had met in combat confronted one another again. Once again, with the cause of justice on our side, we would wage the terrible battle of truth against infamy! Surely the regime was not prepared for the moral catastrophe in store for it!

How could it maintain its false accusations? How keep secret what had really happened, when so many young men were willing to risk everything — prison, torture, and death, if necessary — so that the truth be told before this court?

I was called as a witness at that first session. For two hours I was questioned by the prosecutor as well as by twenty defense attorneys. I was able to prove with exact facts and figures the sums of money that had been spent, the way this money was collected, and the arms we had been able to round up. I had nothing to hide, for the truth was all this was accomplished through sacrifices without precedent in the history of our republic. I spoke of the goals that inspired us in our struggle and of the humane and generous treatment that we had at all times accorded our adversaries. If I accomplished my purpose of demonstrating that those who were falsely implicated in this trial were neither directly nor indirectly involved, I owe it to the complete support and backing of my heroic comrades. For as I said, the consequences they might be forced to suffer at no time caused them to repent of being revolutionaries and patriots. I was never once allowed to speak with these comrades of mine during the time we were in prison, and yet we planned to do exactly the same. The fact is, when men carry the same ideals in their hearts, nothing can isolate them — neither prison walls nor the sod of cemeteries. For a single memory, a single spirit, a single idea, a single conscience, a single dignity will sustain them all.

From that moment on, the structure of lies the regime had erected about the events at Moncada garrison began to collapse like a house of cards. As a result, the prosecutor realized that keeping all those persons named as instigators in prison was completely absurd, and he requested their provisional release.

At the close of my testimony in that first session, I asked the court to allow me to leave the dock and sit among the counsel for the defense. This permission was granted me. At that point what I consider my most important mission in this trial began: to totally discredit the cowardly, miserable, and treacherous lies that the regime had hurled against our fighters; to reveal with irrefutable evidence the horrible, repulsive crimes they had practiced on the prisoners; and to show the nation and the world the infinite misfortune of the Cuban people who are suffering the cruelest, the most inhuman oppression of their history.

The second session convened on Tuesday, September 22. By that time only ten witnesses had testified, and they had already cleared up the murders in the Manzanillo area, specifically establishing and placing on record the direct responsibility of the captain commanding that post. There were three hundred more witnesses to testify. What would have happened if, with a staggering mass of facts and evidence, I had proceeded to cross-examine the very army men who were directly responsible for those crimes? Could the regime have permitted me to go ahead before the large audience attending the trial? Before journalists and jurists from all over the island? And before the party leaders of the opposition, who they had stupidly seated right in the prisoner's dock where they could hear clearly all that might be brought out here? They would rather have blown up the courthouse, with all its judges, than allow that!

And so they devised a plan by which they could eliminate me from the trial and they proceeded to do just that, *manu militari* [by force of arms]. On Friday night, September 25, on the eve of the third session of the trial, two prison doctors visited me in my cell. They were visibly embarrassed. "We have come to examine you," they said. I asked them, "Who is so worried about my health?" Actually, from the moment I saw them I realized what they had come for. They could not have treated me with greater respect, and they explained their predicament to me. That afternoon Colonel Chaviano had appeared at the prison and had told them I "was doing the government terrible damage with this trial." He had told them they must sign a certificate declaring that I was ill and was, therefore, unable to appear in court. The doctors told me that for their part they were prepared to resign from their posts and risk persecution. They put the matter in my hands, for me to decide. I found it hard to ask those men to unhesitatingly destroy themselves. But neither could I, under any circumstances, consent that those orders be carried out. Leaving the matter to their own consciences, I told them only: "You must know your duty; I certainly know mine."

After leaving my cell they signed the certificate. I know they did so believing in good faith that this was the only way they could save my life, which they considered to be in grave danger. I was not obliged to keep our conversation secret, for I am bound only by the truth. Telling the truth in this instance may jeopardize those good doctors in their material interests, but I am removing all doubt about their honor, which is worth much more. That same night, I wrote the court a letter denouncing the plot, requesting that two court physicians be sent to certify my excellent state of health, and to inform you that if to save my life I must take part in such deception, I would a thousand times prefer to lose it. To show my determination to fight alone against this whole degenerate frame-up, I added to my own words one of the Master's lines:[1] "A just cause

even from the depths of a cave can do more than an army."
As the court knows, this was the letter Dr. Melba Hernández submitted at the third session of the trial on September
26. I managed to get it to her in spite of the heavy guard I
was under. That letter, of course, provoked immediate re-
prisals. Dr. Hernández was subjected to solitary confinement and I — since I was already incommunicado — was
sent to the most inaccessible reaches of the prison. From
that moment on, all the accused were thoroughly searched
from head to foot before they were brought into the courtroom.

Two court physicians certified on September 27 that I
was, in fact, in perfect health. Yet in spite of the repeated
orders from the court, I was never again brought to the
hearings. What's more, anonymous persons daily circu-
lated hundreds of apocryphal pamphlets which announced my rescue from jail. This stupid alibi was in-
vented so they could physically eliminate me and pretend
I had tried to escape. Since the scheme failed as a result of
timely exposure by ever-alert friends, and after the first af-
fidavit was shown to be false, the regime could only keep
me away from the trial by open and shameless contempt of
court.

This was an incredible situation, Honorable Judges:
Here was a regime literally afraid to bring an accused
man to court; a regime of blood and terror that shrank
in fear of the moral conviction of a defenseless man —
unarmed, slandered, and isolated. And so, after depriv-
ing me of everything else, they finally deprived me even
of the trial in which I was the main accused. Remember
that this was during a period in which individual rights
were suspended and the Public Order Act as well as
censorship of radio and press were in full force. What
unbelievable crimes this regime must have committed to
so fear the voice of one accused man!

I must dwell upon the insolence and disrespect which
the army leaders have at all times shown toward you. As

often as this court has ordered an end to the inhuman isolation in which I was held; as often as it has ordered my most elementary rights to be respected; as often as it has demanded that I be brought before it, this court has never been obeyed! Worse yet: in the very presence of the court, during the first and second hearings, a praetorian guard was stationed beside me to totally prevent me from speaking to anyone, even during the brief recesses. In other words, not only in prison, but also in the courtroom and in your presence, they ignored your decrees. I had intended to mention this matter in the following session, as a question of elementary respect for the court, but — I was never brought back. And if, in exchange for so much disrespect, they bring us before you to be jailed in the name of a legality which they and they alone have been violating since March 10,[2] sad indeed is the role they would force upon you. The Latin maxim *Cedant arma togae* [Arms should yield to the toga] has certainly not been fulfilled on a single occasion during this trial. I beg you to keep that circumstance well in mind.

What is more, these devices were in any case quite useless; my brave comrades, with unprecedented patriotism, did their duty to the utmost.

"Yes, we set out to fight for Cuba's freedom and we are not ashamed of having done so," they declared, one by one, on the witness stand. Then, addressing the court with impressive courage, they denounced the hideous crimes committed upon the bodies of our brothers. Although absent from court, I was able, in my prison cell, to follow the trial in all its details. And I have the convicts at Boniato Prison to thank for this. In spite of all threats, these men found ingenious means of getting newspaper clippings and all kinds of information to me. In this way they avenged the abuses and immoralities perpetrated against them both by Taboada, the warden, and the supervisor, Lieutenant Rozabal, who drove them from sun up to sun down building private mansions and starved them by embezzling the prison food budget.

As the trial went on, the roles were reversed: those who came to accuse found themselves accused, and the accused became the accusers! It was not the revolutionaries who were judged there; judged once and forever was a man named Batista — *monstrum horrendum* [horrible monster]! And it matters little that these worthy and valiant young men have been condemned, if tomorrow the people will condemn the dictator and his henchmen! Our men were consigned to the Isle of Pines prison, in whose circular galleries Castells's ghost still lingers and where the cries of countless victims still echo; there our young men have been sent to expiate their love of liberty, in bitter confinement, banished from society, torn from their homes, and exiled from their country. Is it not clear to you, as I have said before, that in such circumstances it is difficult and disagreeable for this lawyer to fulfill his duty?

As a result of so many turbid and illegal machinations, due to the will of those who govern and the weakness of those who judge, I find myself here in this little room at the Civilian Hospital, where I have been brought to be tried in secret, so that I may be stifled, and so that no one may learn of the things I am going to say. Why, then, do we need that imposing Palace of Justice which the honorable judges would without doubt find much more comfortable? I must warn you: it is unwise to administer justice from a hospital room, surrounded by sentinels with fixed bayonets; the citizens might suppose that our justice is sick — and that it is captive.

Let me remind you, your laws of procedure provide that trials shall be "public hearings"; however, the people have been barred altogether from this session of court. The only civilians admitted here have been two attorneys and six reporters, in whose newspapers the censorship of the press will prevent printing a word I say. I see, as my sole audience in this chamber and in the corridors, nearly a hundred soldiers and officers. I am grateful for the polite

As an organizer for the Orthodox Party Youth. Poster reads "We look to Chibás."

Left, before 1953 attack on Moncada barracks; right, as prisoner after Moncada.

Under arrest after Moncada.

Police interrogation after Moncada.

Melba Hernández and Haydée Santamaría behind bars in the National Women's Prison in Guanajay.

Title page of first edition of "History Will Absolve Me." In background are title pages of later editions published in Cuba and abroad before 1959.

Release from prison, May 1955.

Target practice in Sierra Maestra 1958.

In the Sierra Maestra.

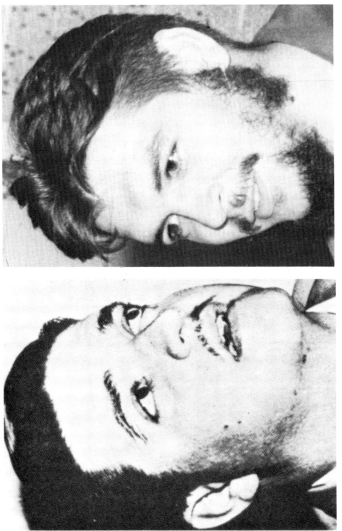

Left, José Antonio Echeverría, General Secretary of Federation of University Students; right, Che Guevara.

Just before the final triumph; Raúl Castro at right.

Negotiating surrender of Santiago de Cuba, December 1958; Celia Sánchez at center.

Entering Havana, January 1959.

With Camilo Cienfuegos, January 1959.

Signing the Agrarian Reform Law, May 1959.

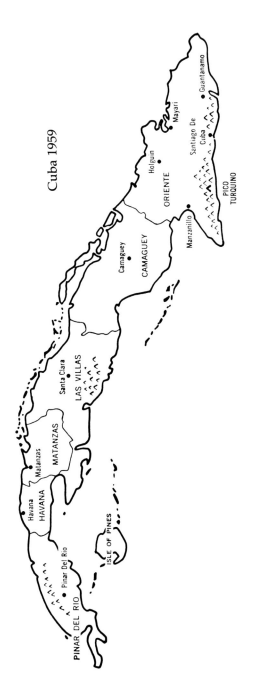

Cuba 1959

Holguin

ORIENTE

Mayari

Santiago De
Cuba

Guantanamo

PICO
TURQUINO

Manzanillo

Camaguey

CAMAGUEY

Santa Clara

LAS VILLAS

Matanzas

MATANZAS

Havana

HAVANA

Pinar Del Rio

PINAR DEL RIO

ISLE OF PINES

and serious attention they give me. I only wish I could have the whole army before me! I know one day this army will seethe with rage to wash away the terrible, the shameful bloodstains splattered across the military uniform by the present ruthless clique in its lust for power. On that day, oh what a fall awaits those mounted in arrogance on their noble steeds! — provided that the people have not dismounted them long before that!

Finally, I should like to add that no treatise on penal law was allowed me in my cell. I have at my disposal only this tiny code of law lent to me by my learned counsel, Dr. Baudilio Castellanos, the courageous defender of my comrades. In the same way they prevented me from receiving the books of Martí; it seems the prison censorship considered them too subversive. Or is it because I said Martí was the inspirer of July 26? Reference books on any other subject were also denied me during this trial. But it makes no difference! I carry the teachings of the Master in my heart, and in my mind the noble ideas of all men who have defended people's freedom everywhere!

I am going to make only one request of this court; I trust it will be granted as a compensation for the many abuses and outrages the accused has had to tolerate without protection of the law. I ask that my right to express myself be respected without restraint. Otherwise, even the merest semblance of justice cannot be maintained, and the final episode of this trial would be, more than all the others, one of ignominy and cowardice.

I must admit that I am somewhat disappointed. I had expected that the honorable prosecutor would come forward with a grave accusation. I thought he would be ready to justify to the limit his contention and his reasons why I should be condemned in the name of law and justice — what law and what justice? — to twenty-six years in prison. But no. He has limited himself to reading Article 148 of the Social Defense Code. On the basis of this, plus aggravating circumstances, he requests that I be impris-

oned for the lengthy term of twenty-six years! Two minutes seems a very short time in which to demand and justify that a man be put behind bars for more than a quarter
of a century. Can it be that the honorable prosecutor is,
perhaps, annoyed with the court? Because as I see it, his
laconic attitude in this case clashes with the solemnity with
which the honorable judges declared, rather proudly, that
this was a trial of the greatest importance! I have heard
prosecutors speak ten times longer in a simple narcotics
case asking a sentence of just six months. The honorable
prosecutor has supplied not a word in support of his petition. I am a just man. I realize that for a prosecuting attorney under oath of loyalty to the constitution of the republic, it is difficult to come here in the name of an unconstitutional, statutory, *de facto* government, lacking any legal
much less moral basis, to ask that a young Cuban, a lawyer
like himself — perhaps as honorable as he — be sent to jail
for twenty-six years. But the honorable prosecutor is a
gifted man and I have seen much less talented persons
write lengthy diatribes in defense of this regime. How then
can I suppose that he lacks reason with which to defend it,
at least for fifteen minutes, however contemptible that
might be to any decent person? It is clear that there is a
great conspiracy behind all this.

Honorable Judges: Why such interest in silencing me?
Why is every type of argument foregone in order to avoid
presenting any target whatsoever against which I might direct my own brief? Is it that they lack any legal, moral, or
political basis on which to put forth a serious formulation
of the question? Are they that afraid of the truth? Do they
hope that I, too, will speak for only two minutes and that I
will not touch upon the points which have caused certain
people sleepless nights since July 26? Since the prosecutor's petition was restricted to the mere reading of five
lines of an article of the Social Defense Code, might they
suppose that I too would limit myself to these same lines
and circle round them like some slave turning a millstone?

I shall by no means accept such a gag, for in this trial there is much more than the freedom of a single individual at stake. Fundamental matters of principle are being debated here, the right of men to be free is on trial, the very foundations of our existence as a civilized and democratic nation are in the balance. When this trial is over, I do not want to have to reproach myself for any principle left undefended, for any truth unsaid, for any crime not denounced.

The honorable prosecutor's famous little article hardly deserves a minute of my time. I shall limit myself for the moment to a brief legal skirmish against it, because I want to clear the field for an assault against all the endless lies and deceits, the hypocrisy, conventionalism, and moral cowardice that have set the stage for the crude comedy which since March 10 — and even before then — has been called justice in Cuba.

It is a fundamental principle of criminal law that an imputed offense must correspond exactly to the type of crime described by law. If no law applies exactly to the point in question, then there is no offense.

The article in question reads textually: "A sentence of three to ten years' imprisonment shall be imposed upon the perpetrator of any act aimed at promoting an armed uprising against the constitutional powers of the state. The sentence shall be five to twenty years' imprisonment if the insurrection actually is carried out."

In what country is the honorable prosecutor living? Who told him that we sought to bring about an uprising against the constitutional powers of the state? Two things are self-evident. First of all, the dictatorship that oppresses the nation is not a constitutional power, but an unconstitutional one: it was established against the constitution, over the head of the constitution, violating the legitimate constitution of the republic. The legitimate constitution is that which emanates directly from a sovereign people. I shall demonstrate this point fully later on, notwithstanding all the subterfuges contrived by cowards and traitors to justify the unjustifiable. Secondly, the article refers to powers, in the plural, as in the case of a republic governed by a legislative power, an executive power, and a judicial power, which balance and counterbalance one another. We have fomented a rebellion against one single power, an illegal one, which has usurped and merged into a single whole both the legislative and executive powers of the nation, and has thus destroyed the entire system that was specifically safeguarded by the code now under our analysis. As to the independence of the judiciary after March 10, I shall not allude to that for I am in no mood for joking. No matter how Article 148 may be stretched, shrunk, or amended, not a single comma applies to the events of July 26. Let us leave this statute alone and await the opportunity to apply it to those who really did foment an uprising against the constitutional powers of the state. Later I shall come back to the code to refresh the honorable prosecutor's memory about certain circumstances he has unfortunately overlooked.

I warn you, I am just beginning! If there is in your hearts a vestige of love for your country, love for humanity, love for justice, listen carefully. I know that I will be silenced for many years; I know that the regime will try to suppress the truth by all possible means; I know that there will be a conspiracy to bury me in oblivion. But my voice will not be stilled — it will rise from my breast even when I feel most alone, and my heart will give it all the fire that callous cowards deny it.

3

From a shack in the mountains on Monday, July 27, I listened to the dictator's voice on the air while there were still eighteen of our men in arms against the government. Those who have never experienced similar moments will never know that kind of bitterness and indignation. While the long-cherished hopes of freeing our people lay in ruins about us, we heard those crushed hopes gloated over by a tyrant more vicious, more arrogant than ever. The endless stream of lies and slanders, poured forth in his crude, odious, repulsive language, may only be compared to the endless stream of clean young blood which had flowed since the previous night — with his knowledge, consent, complicity, and approval — being spilled by the most inhuman gang of assassins it is possible to imagine. To have believed him for a single moment would have sufficed to fill a man of conscience with remorse and shame for the rest of his life. At that time I could not even hope to brand his miserable forehead with the mark of truth which condemns him for the rest of his days and for all time to come. Already a circle of more than a thousand men, armed with weapons more powerful than ours and with peremptory orders to bring in our bodies, was closing in around us. Now that the truth is coming out, now that speaking before you I am carrying out the mission I set for myself, I may die peacefully and content. So I shall not mince any words about those savage murderers.

I must pause to consider the facts for a moment. The government itself said the attack showed such precision and perfection that it must have been planned by military strategists. Nothing could have been farther from the truth! The plan was drawn up by a group of young men, none of whom had any military experience at all. I will reveal their names, omitting two who are neither dead nor in prison: Abel Santamaría, José Luis Tasende, Renato Guitart Rosell, Pedro Miret, Jesús Montané, and myself. Half of them are dead, and in tribute to their memory I can say that although they were not military experts they had enough patriotism to have given, had we not been at such a great disadvantage, a good beating to that entire lot of generals together, those generals of March 10 who are neither soldiers nor patriots. Much more difficult than the planning of the attack was our organizing, training, mobilizing, and arming men under this repressive regime with its millions of dollars spent on espionage, bribery, and information services. Nevertheless, all this was carried out by those men and many others like them with incredible seriousness, discretion, and discipline. Still more praiseworthy is the fact that they gave this task everything they had; ultimately, their very lives.

The final mobilization of men who came to this province from the most remote towns of the entire island was accomplished with admirable precision and in absolute secrecy. It is equally true that the attack was carried out with magnificent coordination. It began simultaneously at 5:15 a.m. in both Bayamo and Santiago de Cuba; and one by one, with an exactitude of minutes and seconds prepared in advance, the buildings surrounding the barracks fell to our forces. Nevertheless, in the interest of truth and even though it may detract from our merit, I am also going to reveal for the first time a fact that was fatal: due to a most unfortunate error, half of our forces, and the better armed half at that, went astray at the entrance to the city and were not on hand to help us at the decisive moment. Abel Santamaría, with twenty-one men, had occupied the Civilian Hospital; with him went a doctor and two of our women comrades to attend to the wounded. Raúl Castro, with ten men, occupied the Palace of Justice, and it was my responsibility to attack the barracks with the rest, ninety-five men. Preceded by an advance group of eight who had forced gate three, I arrived with the first group of forty-five men. It was precisely here that the battle began, when my car ran into an outside patrol armed with machine guns. The reserve group, which had almost all the heavy weapons (the light arms were with the advance group), turned up the wrong street and lost its way in an unfamiliar city. I must clarify the fact that I do not have the least doubt about the courage of those men: they experienced great anguish and desperation when they realized they were lost. Because of the type of action it was and because the contending forces were wearing identically colored uniforms, it was not easy for these men to reestablish contact with us. Many of them, captured later on, met death with true heroism.

Everyone had instructions, first of all, to be humane in the struggle. Never was a group of armed men more generous to the adversary. From the beginning we took numerous prisoners — nearly twenty — and there was one moment when three of our men — Ramiro Valdés, José Suárez, and Jesús Montané — managed to enter a barracks and hold nearly fifty soldiers prisoners for a short time. Those soldiers testified before the court, and without exception they all acknowledged that we treated them with absolute respect, that we didn't even subject them to one scoffing remark. In line with this, I want to give my heartfelt thanks to the prosecutor for one thing in the trial of my comrades: when he made his report he was fair enough to acknowledge as an incontestable fact that we maintained a high spirit of chivalry throughout the struggle.

Discipline among the soldiers was very poor. They finally defeated us because of their superior numbers — fifteen to one — and because of the protection afforded them by the defense of the fortress. Our men were much better marksmen, as our enemies themselves conceded. There was a high degree of courage on both sides.

In analyzing the reasons for our tactical failure, apart from the regrettable error already mentioned, I believe we made a mistake by dividing the commando unit we had so carefully trained. Of our best trained men and boldest leaders, there were twenty-seven in Bayamo, twenty-one at the Civilian Hospital, and ten at the Palace of Justice. If our forces had been distributed differently the outcome of the battle might have been different. The clash with the patrol (purely accidental, since the unit might have been at that point twenty seconds earlier or twenty seconds later) alerted the camp and gave it time to mobilize. Otherwise the camp would have fallen into our hands without a shot fired, since we already controlled the guard post. On the other hand, except for the .22 caliber rifles, for which there were plenty of bullets, our side was very short of ammunition. Had we had hand grenades the army would not have been able to resist us for fifteen minutes.

When I became convinced that all efforts to take the barracks were now useless, I began to withdraw our men in groups of eight and ten. Our retreat was covered by six expert marksmen under the command of Pedro Miret and Fidel Labrador; heroically they held off the army's advance. Our losses in the battle had been insignificant; 95 percent of our casualties came from the army's inhumanity after the struggle. The group at the Civilian Hospital had only one casualty; the rest of that group was trapped when the troops blocked the only exit; but our youths did not lay down their arms until their very last bullet was gone. With them was Abel Santamaría, the most generous, beloved, and intrepid of our young men, whose glorious resistance immortalizes him in Cuban history. We shall see the fate they met and how Batista sought to punish the heroism of our youth.

We planned to continue the struggle in the mountains in case the attack on the regiment failed. In Siboney I was able to gather a third of our forces; but many of these men were now discouraged. About twenty of them decided to surrender; later we shall see what became of them. The rest, eighteen men, with what arms and ammunition were left, followed me into the mountains. The terrain was completely unknown to us. For a week we held the heights of the Gran Piedra range and the army occupied the foothills. We could not come down; they didn't risk coming up. It was not force of arms, but hunger and thirst that ultimately overcame our resistance. I had to divide the men into smaller groups. Some of them managed to slip through the army lines; others were surrendered by Monsignor Pérez Serantes. Finally only two comrades remained with me — José Suárez and Oscar Alcalde. While the three of us were totally exhausted, a force led by Lieutenant Sarría surprised us in our sleep at dawn. This was Saturday, August 1. By that time the slaughter of prisoners had ceased, as a result of the tremendous reaction it had provoked in the citizenry. This officer, a man of honor, saved us from being murdered on the spot with our hands tied behind us.

I need not deny here the stupid statements by Ugalde Carrillo and company, who tried to stain my name in an effort to mask their own cowardice, incompetence, and criminality. The facts are clear enough.

My purpose is not to bore the court with epic narratives. All that I have said is essential for a more precise understanding of what is yet to come.

Let me mention two important facts that facilitate an objective judgment of our attitude. First: we could have taken over the ranking officers in their homes. This possibility was rejected for the very humane reason that we wished to avoid scenes of tragedy and struggle in the presence of their families. Second: we decided not to take over any radio station until the army camp was in our power. This attitude, unusually magnanimous and considerate, spared the citizens a great deal of bloodshed. With only ten men I could have seized a radio station and called the people to revolt. There is no question of the people's will to fight. I had a recording of Eduardo Chibás's last message over the CMQ radio network and patriotic poems and battle hymns capable of moving the least sensitive, especially with the sounds of live battle in their ears. But I did not want to use them although our situation was desperate.

4

The regime has stated over and over that our movement did not have popular support. I have never heard an assertion so naive and at the same time so full of bad faith. The regime seeks to show submission and cowardice on the part of the people. They all but claim that the people support the dictatorship; they do not know how offensive this is to the brave *Orientales*. Santiago thought our attack was only a local disturbance between two factions of soldiers; not until many hours later did they realize what had really happened. Who can doubt the valor, civic pride, and limitless courage of the rebel and patriotic people of Santiago de Cuba? If Moncada had fallen into our hands, even the women of Santiago de Cuba would have risen in arms. Many were the rifles loaded for our fighters by the nurses at the Civilian Hospital. They fought alongside us. That is something we will never forget.

It was never our intention to engage the soldiers of the regiment in combat. We wanted to seize control of them and their weapons in a surprise attack, arouse the people, and call on the soldiers to abandon the odious flag of the tyranny and to embrace the banner of freedom; to defend the supreme interests of the nation and not the petty interests of a small clique; to turn their guns around and fire on the people's enemies and not on the people, among whom are their own sons and fathers; to unite with the people as the brothers that they are instead of opposing the people as the enemies the government tries to make of them; to march behind the only beautiful ideal worthy of sacrificing one's life for — the greatness and happiness of one's country. To those who doubt that many soldiers would have followed us, I ask: What Cuban does not cherish glory? What heart is not set aflame by the promise of freedom?

The navy did not fight against us, and it would undoubtedly have come over to our side later on. It is well known that that branch of the armed forces is the least dominated by the dictatorship and that there is a very intense civic conscience among its members. But, as to the rest of the national armed forces, would they have fought against a people in revolt? I declare that they would not! A soldier is made of flesh and blood; he thinks, observes, feels. He is susceptible to the opinions, beliefs, sympathies, and antipathies of the people. If you ask his opinion, he may tell you he cannot express it; but that does not mean he has no opinion. He is affected by exactly the same problems that affect other citizens — subsistence, rent, the education of his children, their future, etc. Everything of this kind is an inevitable point of contact between him and the people, and everything of this kind relates him to the present and future situation of the society in which he lives. It is foolish to imagine that the salary a soldier receives from the state — a modest enough salary, at that — should solve the vital problems imposed on him by his needs, duties, and feelings as a member of his family and as a member of his community.

This brief explanation has been necessary because it is basic to a consideration to which few people, until now, have paid any attention — soldiers have a deep respect for the feelings of the majority of the people! During the Machado regime, in the same proportion as popular antipathy increased, the loyalty of the army visibly decreased. This was so true that a group of women almost succeeded in subverting Camp Columbia. But this is proved even more clearly by a recent development. While Grau San Martín's regime was able to preserve its maximum popularity among the people, unscrupulous ex-officers and power-hungry civilians attempted innumerable conspiracies in the army, but none of them found a following in the rank and file.

The March 10 coup took place at the moment when the civil government's prestige had dwindled to its lowest ebb, a circumstance of which Batista and his clique took advantage. Why did they not strike their blow after June 1? Simply because, had they waited for the majority of the nation to express its will at the polls, the troops would not have responded to the conspiracy!

Consequently, a second assertion can be made: the army has never revolted against a regime with a popular majority behind it. These are historic truths, and if Batista insists on remaining in power at all costs against the will of the majority of Cubans, his end will be more tragic than that of Gerardo Machado.

I have a right to express an opinion about the armed forces, because I defended them when everyone else was silent. And I did this neither as a conspirator nor from any kind of personal interest — for we then enjoyed full constitutional prerogatives. I was prompted only by humane instincts and civic duty. In those days, the newspaper *Alerta* was one of the most widely read because of its position on national political matters. In its pages, I campaigned against the forced labor to which the soldiers were subjected on the private estates of high personages and military officers. On March 3, 1952, I supplied the courts with data, photographs, films, and other proof denouncing this state of affairs. I also pointed out in those articles that it was elementary decency to increase army salaries. I should like to know who else raised his voice on that occasion to protest against all this injustice done the soldiers. Certainly not Batista and company, living well protected on their luxurious estates, surrounded by all kinds of security measures, while I ran a thousand risks with neither bodyguards nor arms.

Just as I defended the soldiers then, now — when all others are once more silent — I tell them that they allowed themselves to be miserably deceived; and to the deception and shame of March 10, they have added the disgrace, the thousand times greater disgrace, of the fearful and unjustifiable crimes of Santiago de Cuba. From that time since, the uniform of the army is spattered with blood. And as last year I told the people and cried out before the courts that soldiers were working as slaves on private estates, today I make the bitter charge that there are soldiers stained from head to toe with the blood of the Cuban youths they have tortured and slain. And I say as well that if the army serves the republic, defends the nation, respects the people, and protects the citizenry then it is only fair that the soldier should earn at least a hundred pesos a month. But if the soldiers slay and oppress the people, betray the nation, and defend only the interests of one small group, then the army deserves not a cent of the republic's money, and Camp Columbia should be converted into a school with ten thousand orphans living there instead of soldiers.

I want to be just above everything else, so I can't blame all the soldiers for the shameful crimes that stain a few evil and treacherous army men. But every honorable and upstanding soldier who loves his career and his uniform is duty bound to demand and to fight for the cleansing of this guilt, to avenge this betrayal, and to see the guilty punished. Otherwise the soldier's uniform will forever be a mark of infamy instead of a source of pride.

Of course the March 10 regime had no choice but to remove the soldiers from the private estates. But it did so only to put them to work as doormen, chauffeurs, servants, and bodyguards for the whole rabble of petty politicians who make up the party of the dictatorship. Every fourth- or fifth-rank official considers himself entitled to the services of a soldier to drive his car and to watch over him as if he were constantly afraid of receiving the kick in the pants he so justly deserves.

If they had been at all interested in promoting real reforms, why did the regime not confiscate the estates and the millions of men like Genovevo Pérez Dámera, who acquired their fortunes by exploiting soldiers, driving them like slaves, and misappropriating the funds of the armed forces? But no: Genovevo Pérez and others like him no doubt still have soldiers protecting them on their estates, because the March 10 generals, deep in their hearts, aspire to the same future and can't allow that kind of precedent to be set.

March 10 was a miserable deception, yes. After Batista and his band of corrupt and disreputable politicians had failed in their electoral plan, they took advantage of the army's discontent and used it to climb to power on the backs of the soldiers. And I know there are many army men who are disgusted because they have been disappointed. At first their pay was raised, but later, through deductions and reductions of every kind, it was lowered again. Many of the old elements, who had drifted away from the armed forces, returned to the ranks and blocked the way of young, capable, and valuable men who might otherwise have advanced. Good soldiers have been neglected while the most scandalous nepotism prevails. Many decent military men are now asking themselves what need the armed forces had to assume the tremendous historical responsibility of destroying our constitution merely to put a group of immoral men in power, men of bad reputation, corrupt, politically degenerate beyond redemption, who could never again have occupied a political post had it not been at bayonet point; and they weren't even the ones with the bayonets in their hands.

On the other hand, the soldiers endure a worse tyranny than the civilians. They are under constant surveillance and not one of them enjoys the slightest security in his job. Any unjustified suspicion, any gossip, any intrigue or denunciation, is sufficient to bring transfer, dishonorable discharge, or imprisonment. Did not Tabernilla, in a memorandum, forbid them to talk with anyone opposed to the government, that is to say, with 99 percent of the people? What a lack of confidence! Not even the vestal virgins of Rome had to abide by such a rule! As for the much publicized little houses for enlisted men, there aren't 300 on the whole island; yet with what has been spent on tanks, guns, and other weaponry every soldier might have a place to live.

Batista isn't concerned with taking care of the army, but with the army taking care of him! He increases the army's power of oppression and killing but does not improve the living conditions for the soldiers. Triple guard duty, constant confinement to the barracks, continuous anxiety, the enmity of the people, uncertainty about the future — this is what has been given to the soldier. In other words: "Die for the regime, soldier, give it your sweat and blood. We shall dedicate a speech to you and award you a posthumous promotion (when it no longer matters) and afterwards . . . we shall go on living luxuriously, making ourselves rich. Kill, abuse, oppress the people. When the people get tired and all this comes to an end, you can pay for our crimes while we go abroad and live like kings. And if one day we return, don't you or your children knock on the doors of our mansions, for we shall be millionaires and millionaires do not mingle with the poor. Kill, soldier, oppress the people, die for the regime, give your sweat and blood. . . ."

But if blind to this sad truth, a minority of soldiers had decided to fight the people, the people who were going to liberate them from tyranny, victory still would have gone to the people.

5

The honorable prosecutor was very interested in knowing our chances for success. These chances were based on considerations of technical, military, and social order. They have tried to establish the myth that modern arms render the people helpless in overthrowing tyrants. Military parades and the pompous display of the machines of war are used to perpetuate this myth and to create a complex of absolute impotence in the people. But no weaponry, no violence can vanquish the people once they are determined to win back their rights. Both past and present are full of examples. The most recent is the revolt in Bolivia, where miners with dynamite sticks smashed and defeated regular army regiments.

Fortunately, we Cubans need not look for examples abroad. No example is as inspiring as that of our own land. During the war of 1895 there were nearly half a million armed Spanish soldiers in Cuba, many more than the dictator counts upon today to hold back a population five times greater. The arms of the Spaniards were, incomparably, both more up to date and more powerful than those of our *mambises*.[3] Often the Spaniards were equipped with field artillery and the infantry used breechloaders similar to those still in use by the infantry of today. The Cubans were usually armed with no more than their *machetes*, for their cartridge belts were almost always empty. There is an unforgettable passage in the history of our war of independence, narrated by Gen. Miró Argenter, chief of Antonio Maceo's general staff. I managed to bring it copied on this scrap of paper so I wouldn't have to depend upon my memory:

"Untrained men under the command of Pedro Delgado, most of them equipped only with *machetes*, were virtually annihilated as they threw themselves on the solid rank of Spaniards with their bare fists, without machetes, without even knives. Searching through the reeds by the Hondo River, we found fifteen more dead from the Cuban party, and it was not immediately clear what group they belonged to. They did not appear to have shouldered arms, their clothes were intact and only tin drinking cups hung from their waists; a few steps farther on lay the dead horse, all its equipment in order. We reconstructed the climax of the tragedy. These men, following their daring chief, Lieutenant Colonel Pedro Delgado, had earned heroes' laurels: they had thrown themselves against bayonets with bare hands, the clash of metal which was heard around them was the sound of their drinking cups banging against the saddlehorn. Maceo was deeply moved. This man so used to seeing death in all its forms murmured this praise: 'I had never seen anything like this, untrained and unarmed men attacking the Spaniards with only a drinking cup for a weapon. And I called it impedimenta!' "

This is how people fight when they want to win their freedom; they throw stones at airplanes and overturn tanks!

As soon as Santiago de Cuba was in our hands we would immediately have readied the people of Oriente for war. Bayamo was attacked precisely to locate our advance forces along the Cauto River. Never forget that this province, which has a million and a half inhabitants today, is the most rebellious and patriotic in Cuba. It was this province that sparked the fight for independence for thirty years and paid the highest price in blood, sacrifice, and heroism. In Oriente you can still breathe the air of that glorious epic. At dawn, when the cocks crow as if they were bugles calling soldiers to reveille, and when the sun rises radiant over the rugged mountains, it seems that once again we will live the days of Yara or Baire![4]

6

I stated that the second consideration on which we based our chances for success was one of social order. Why were we sure of the people's support? When we speak of the people we are not talking about those who live in comfort, the conservative elements of the nation, who welcome any oppressive regime, any dictatorship, any despotism — prostrating themselves before the masters of the moment until they grind their foreheads into the ground. When we speak of struggle and we mention the people, we mean the vast unredeemed masses, those to whom everyone makes promises and who are deceived by all; we mean the people who yearn for a better, more dignified, and more just nation; those who are moved by ancestral aspirations of justice, for they have suffered injustice and mockery generation after generation; those who long for great and wise changes in all aspects of their life; people who, to attain those changes, are ready to give even the very last breath they have, when they believe in something or in someone, especially when they believe in themselves. The first condition of sincerity and good faith in any endeavor is to do precisely what nobody else ever does, that is, to speak with absolute clarity, without fear. The demagogues and professional politicians who manage to perform the miracle of being right about everything and of pleasing everyone are, necessarily, deceiving everyone about everything. The revolutionaries must proclaim their ideas courageously, define their principles, and express their intentions so that no one is deceived, neither friend nor foe.

In terms of struggle, when we talk about people we're talking about the *six hundred thousand* Cubans without work, who want to earn their daily bread honestly without having to emigrate from their homeland in search of a livelihood; the *five hundred thousand* farm laborers who live in miserable shacks, who work four months of the year and starve the rest, sharing their misery with their children, who don't have an inch of land to till and whose existence would move any heart not made of stone; the *four hundred thousand* industrial workers and laborers whose retirement funds have been embezzled, whose benefits are being taken away, whose homes are wretched quarters, whose salaries pass from the hands of the boss to those of the moneylender, whose future is a pay reduction and dismissal, whose life is endless work and whose only rest is the tomb; the *one hundred thousand* small farmers who live and die working land that is not theirs, looking at it with the sadness of Moses gazing at the promised land, to die without ever owning it, who like feudal serfs have to pay for the use of their parcel of land by giving up a portion of its produce, who cannot love it, improve it, beautify it, nor plant a cedar or an orange tree on it because they never know when a sheriff will come with the rural guard to evict them from it; the *thirty thousand* teachers and professors who are so devoted, dedicated, and so necessary to the better destiny of future generations and who are so badly treated and paid; the *twenty thousand* small businessmen weighed down by debts, ruined by the crisis, and harangued by a plague of grafting and venal officials; the *ten thousand* young professional people: doctors, engineers, lawyers, veterinarians, school teachers, dentists, pharmacists, newspapermen, painters, sculptors, etc., who finish school with their degrees, anxious to work and full of hope, only to find themselves at a dead end, all doors closed to them, and where no ear hears their clamor or supplication. These are the people, the ones who know misfortune and, therefore, are capable of fighting with limitless courage! To these people whose desperate roads through life have been paved with the bricks of betrayal and false promises, we were not going to say: "We will give you . . . " but rather: "Here it is, now fight for it with everything you have, so that liberty and happiness may be yours!"

7

The five revolutionary laws that would have been proclaimed immediately after the capture of the Moncada garrison and would have been broadcast to the nation by radio must be included in the indictment. It is possible that Colonel Chaviano may have deliberately destroyed these documents, but even if he has I remember them.

The first revolutionary law would have returned the power to the people and proclaimed the 1940 constitution the supreme law of the state until such time as the people should decide to modify or change it. And in order to effect its implementation and punish those who violated it — there being no electoral organization to carry this out — the revolutionary movement, as the circumstantial incarnation of this sovereignty, the only source of legitimate power, would have assumed all the faculties inherent therein, except that of modifying the constitution itself: in other words, it would have assumed the legislative, executive, and judicial powers.

This attitude could not be clearer nor more free of vacillation and sterile charlatanry. A government acclaimed by the mass of rebel people would be vested with every power, everything necessary in order to proceed with the effective implementation of popular will and real justice. From that moment, the judicial power — which since March 10 had placed itself against and outside the constitution — would cease to exist and we would proceed to its immediate and total reform before it would once again assume the power granted it by the supreme law of the republic. Without these previous measures, a return to legality by putting its custody back into the hands that have crippled the system so dishonorably would constitute a fraud, a deceit, one more betrayal.

The second revolutionary law would give nonmortgageable and nontransferable ownership of the land to all tenant and subtenant farmers, lessees, sharecroppers, and squatters who hold parcels of five *caballerías* of land or less,[5] and the state would indemnify the former owners on the basis of the rental which they would have received for these parcels over a period of ten years.

The third revolutionary law would have granted workers and employees the right to share 30 percent of the profits of all large industrial, mercantile, and mining enterprises, including the sugar mills. The strictly agricultural enterprises would be exempt in consideration of other agrarian laws which would be put into effect.

The fourth revolutionary law would have granted all sugar planters the right to share 55 percent of the sugar production and a minimum quota of forty thousand *arrobas* for all small tenant farmers who have been established for three years or more.

The fifth revolutionary law would have ordered the confiscation of all holdings and ill-gotten gains of those who had committed fraud during previous regimes, as well as the holdings and ill-gotten gains of all their legates and heirs. To implement this, special courts with full powers would gain access to all records of all corporations registered or operating in this country, in order to investigate concealed funds of illegal origin and to request that foreign governments extradite persons and attach holdings rightfully belonging to the Cuban people. Half of the property recovered would be used to subsidize retirement funds for workers and the other half would be used for hospitals, asylums, and charitable organizations.

Furthermore, it was to be declared that the Cuban policy in the Americas would be one of close solidarity with the democratic peoples of this continent, and that all those politically persecuted by bloody tyrannies oppressing our sister nations would find generous asylum, brotherhood, and bread in the land of Martí; not the persecution, hunger, and treason they find today. Cuba should be the bulwark of liberty and not a shameful link in the chain of despotism.

These laws would have been proclaimed immediately. As soon as the upheaval ended and prior to a detailed and far-reaching study, they would have been followed by another series of laws and fundamental measures, such as the agrarian reform, the integral educational reform, nationalization of the electric power trust and the telephone trust, refund to the people of the illegal excessive rates these companies have charged, and payment to the treasury of all taxes brazenly evaded in the past.

All these laws and others would be based on exact compliance with two essential articles of our constitution: one of them orders the outlawing of large estates, indicating the maximum area of land any one person or entity may own for each type of agricultural enterprise, by adopting measures which would tend to revert the land to the Cubans. The other categorically orders the state to use all means at its disposal to provide employment for all those who lack it and to insure a decent livelihood to each manual or intellectual laborer. None of these laws can be called unconstitutional. The first popularly elected government would have to respect them, not only because of moral obligations to the nation, but because when people achieve something they have yearned for throughout generations, no force in the world is capable of taking it away again.

The problem of the land, the problem of industrialization, the problem of housing, the problem of unemployment, the problem of education, and the problem of the people's health: these are the six problems we would take immediate steps to solve, along with restoration of civil liberties and political democracy.

This exposition may seem cold and theoretical if one does not know the shocking and tragic conditions of the country with regard to these six problems, along with the most humiliating political oppression.

Eighty-five percent of the small farmers in Cuba pay rent and live under the constant threat of being evicted from the land they till. More than half of our most productive land is in the hands of foreigners. In Oriente, the largest province, the lands of the United Fruit Company link the northern and southern coasts. There are *two hundred thousand peasant families* who do not have a single acre of land to till to provide food for their starving children. On the other hand, nearly *three hundred thousand caballerías* of cultivable land owned by powerful interests remain uncultivated. If Cuba is above all an agricultural state, if its population is largely rural, if the city depends on these rural areas, if the people from our countryside won our war of independence, if our nation's greatness and prosperity depend on a healthy and vigorous rural population that loves the land and knows how to work it, if this population depends on a state that protects and guides it, then how can the present state of affairs be allowed to continue?

Except for a few food, lumber, and textile industries, Cuba continues to be primarily a producer of raw materials. We export sugar to import candy, we export hides to import shoes, we export iron to import plows. Everyone agrees with the urgent need to industrialize the nation, that we need steel industries, paper and chemical industries, that we must improve our cattle and grain production, the technique and the processing in our food industry in order to defend ourselves against the ruinous competition of the Europeans in cheese products, condensed milk, liquors, and edible oils, and of the United States in canned goods; that we need cargo ships; that tourism should be an enormous source of revenue. But the capitalists insist that the workers remain under the yoke. The state sits back with its arms crossed and industrialization can wait forever.

Just as serious or even worse is the housing problem. There are *two hundred thousand* huts and hovels in Cuba; *four hundred thousand* families in the countryside and in the cities live cramped in huts and tenements without even the minimum sanitary requirements; *two million two hundred thousand* of our urban population pay rents which absorb between one fifth and one third of their incomes; and *two million eight hundred thousand* of our rural and suburban population lack electricity. We have the same situation here: if the state proposes the lowering of rents, landlords threaten to freeze all construction; if the state does not interfere, construction goes on so long as the landlords get high rents; otherwise they would not lay a single brick even though the rest of the population had to live totally exposed to the elements. The utilities monopoly is no better; they extend lines as far as it is profitable and beyond that point they don't care if people have to live in darkness for the rest of their lives. The state sits back with its arms crossed, and the people have neither homes nor electricity.

Our educational system is perfectly compatible with everything I've just mentioned. Where the peasant doesn't own the land, what need is there for agricultural schools? Where there is no industry, what need is there for technological or vocational schools? Everything follows the same absurd logic; if we don't have one thing we can't have the other. In any small European country there are more than 200 technological and vocational schools; in Cuba only six such schools exist, and the graduates have no jobs for their skills. The little rural schoolhouses are attended by a mere half of the school-age children — barefooted, half-naked, and undernourished — and frequently the teacher must buy necessary school materials from his own salary. Is this the way to make a nation great?

Only death can liberate one from so much misery. In this respect, however, the state is most helpful — in providing early death for the people. *Ninety percent* of the children in the countryside are consumed by parasites which filter through their bare feet from the ground they walk on. Society is moved to compassion when it hears of the kidnapping or murder of one child, but it is criminally indifferent to the mass murder of so many thousands of children who die every year from lack of facilities, agonizing with pain. Their innocent eyes, death already shining in them, seem to look into some vague infinity as if entreating forgiveness for human selfishness, as if asking God to stay wrath. And when the head of a family works only four months a year, with what can he purchase clothing and medicine for his children? They will grow up with rickets, with not a single good tooth in their mouths by the time they reach thirty; they will have heard ten million speeches and will finally die of misery and deception. Public hospitals, which are always full, accept only patients recommended by some powerful politician who, in turn, demands the electoral votes of the unfortunate one and his family so that Cuba may continue forever in the same or worse condition.

With this background, is it not understandable that from May to December over a million persons are jobless and that Cuba, with a population of five and a half million, has a greater number of unemployed than France or Italy with a population of forty million each?

When you try a defendant for robbery, Honorable Judges, do you ask him how long he has been unemployed? Do you ask him how many children he has, which days of the week he ate and which he didn't; do you investigate his social context at all? You just send him to jail without further thought. But those who burn warehouses and stores to collect insurance do not go to jail, even though a few human beings may have gone up in flames. The insured have money to hire lawyers and bribe judges. You imprison the poor wretch who steals because he is hungry; but none of the hundreds who steal millions from the government has ever spent a night in jail. You dine with them at the end of the year in some elegant club and they enjoy your respect. In Cuba, when a government official becomes a millionaire overnight and enters the fraternity of the rich, he could very well be greeted with the words of that opulent character out of Balzac — Taillerfer — who in his toast to the young heir to an enormous fortune, said: "Gentlemen, let us drink to the power of gold! Mr. Valentine, a millionaire six times over, has just ascended the throne. He is king, can do everything, is above everyone, as all the rich are. Henceforth, equality before the law, established by the constitution, will be a myth for him; for he will not be subject to laws: the laws will be subject to him. There are no courts nor are there sentences for millionaires."

The nation's future, the solutions to its problems, cannot continue to depend on the selfish interests of a dozen big businessmen nor on the cold calculations of profits that ten or twelve magnates draw up in their air-conditioned offices. The country cannot continue begging on its knees for miracles from a few golden calves, like the biblical one destroyed by the prophet's fury. Golden calves cannot perform miracles of any kind. The problems of the republic can be solved only if we dedicate ourselves to fight for it with the same energy, honesty, and patriotism our liberators had when they founded it. Statesmen like Carlos Saladrigas, whose statesmanship consists of preserving the status quo and mouthing phrases like "absolute freedom of enterprise," "guarantees to investment capital," and "the law of supply and demand," will not solve these problems. Those ministers can chat away in a Fifth Avenue mansion until not even the dust of the bones of those whose problems require immediate solution remains. In this present-day world, social problems are not solved by spontaneous generation.

A revolutionary government backed by the people and with the respect of the nation, after cleansing the different institutions of all venal and corrupt officials, would proceed immediately to the country's industrialization, mobilizing all inactive capital, currently estimated at about 1.5 billion pesos, through the National Bank and the Agricultural and Industrial Development Bank, and submitting this mammoth task to experts and men of absolute competence totally removed from all political machines, for study, direction, planning, and realization.

After settling the one hundred thousand small farmers as owners on the land which they previously rented, a revolutionary government would immediately proceed to settle the land problem. First, as set forth in the constitution, it would establish the maximum amount of land to be held by each type of agricultural enterprise and would acquire the excess acreage by expropriation, recovery of the lands stolen from the state, improvement of swampland, planting of large nurseries, and reserving of zones for reforestation. Second, it would distribute the remaining land among peasant families with priority given to the larger ones and would promote agricultural cooperatives for communal use of expensive equipment, freezing plants, and single technical, professional guidelines in farming and cattle raising. Finally, it would provide resources, equipment, protection, and useful guidance to the peasants.

A revolutionary government would solve the housing problem by cutting all rents in half, by providing tax exemptions on homes inhabited by the owners; by tripling taxes on rented homes; by tearing down hovels and replacing them with modern apartment buildings; and by financing housing all over the island on a scale heretofore unheard of, with the criterion that, just as each rural family should possess its own tract of land, each city family should own its own home or apartment. There is plenty of building material and more than enough manpower to make a decent home for every Cuban. But if we continue to wait for the golden calf, a thousand years will have gone by and the problem will remain the same. On the other hand, today possibilities of taking electricity to the most isolated areas on the island are greater than ever. The use of nuclear energy in this field is now a reality and will greatly reduce the cost of producing electricity.

With these three projects and reforms, the problem of unemployment would automatically disappear and the task of improving public health and fighting against disease would become much less difficult.

Finally, a revolutionary government would undertake the integral reform of the educational system, bringing it into line with the projects just mentioned with the idea of educating those generations which will have the privilege of living in a happier land. Do not forget the words of the Apostle:[6] "A grave mistake is being made in Latin America: in countries that live almost completely from the produce of the land, men are being educated exclusively for urban life and are not trained for farm life." "The happiest country is the one which has best educated its sons, both in the instruction of thought and the direction of their feelings." "An educated country will always be strong and free."

8

The soul of education, however, is the teacher, and in Cuba the teaching profession is miserably underpaid. Despite this, no one is more dedicated than the Cuban teacher. Who among us has not learned his ABC's in the little public schoolhouse? It is time we stopped paying pittances to these young men and women who are entrusted with the sacred task of teaching our youth. No teacher should earn less than 200 pesos, no secondary teacher should make less than 350 pesos if they are to devote themselves exclusively to their high calling without suffering want. What is more, all rural teachers should have free use of the various systems of transportation; and, at least once every five years, all teachers should enjoy a sabbatical leave of six months with pay so they may attend special refresher courses at home or abroad to keep abreast of the latest developments in their field. In this way, the curriculum and the teaching system can be constantly improved. Where will the money be found for all this? When there is an end to the embezzlement of government funds, when public officials stop taking graft from the large companies that owe taxes to the state, when the enormous resources of the country are brought into full use, when we no longer buy tanks, bombers, and guns for this country (which has no frontiers to defend and where these instruments of war, now being purchased, are used against the people), when there is more interest in educating the people than in killing them, there will be more than enough money.

Cuba could easily provide for a population three times as great as it has now, so there is no excuse for the abject poverty of a single one of its present inhabitants. The markets should be overflowing with produce, pantries should be full, all hands should be working. This is not an inconceivable thought. What is inconceivable is that anyone should go to bed hungry while there is a single inch of unproductive land, that children should die for lack of medical attention. What is inconceivable is that 30 percent of our farm people cannot write their names and that 99 percent of them know nothing of Cuba's history. What is inconceivable is that the majority of our rural people are now living in worse circumstances than the Indians Columbus discovered in the fairest land that human eyes had ever seen.

To those who would call me a dreamer, I quote the

words of Martí: "A true man does not seek the path where advantage lies, but rather the path where duty lies, and this is the only practical man, whose dream of today will be the law of tomorrow, because he who has looked back on the essential course of history and has seen flaming and bleeding peoples seethe in the cauldron of the ages knows that, without a single exception, the future lies on the side of duty."

Only when we understand that such a high ideal inspired them, can we conceive of the heroism of the young men who fell in Santiago. The meager material means at our disposal was all that prevented sure success. When the soldiers were told that Prío had given us a million pesos, they were told this in the regime's attempt to distort the most important fact: the fact that our movement had no link with past politicians, that this movement is a new Cuban generation with its own ideas, rising up against tyranny; that this movement is made up of young men who were barely seven years old when Batista perpetrated the first of his crimes in 1934. The lie about the million pesos could not have been more absurd. If, with less than 20,000 pesos, we armed 165 men and attacked a regiment and a squadron, then with a million pesos we could have armed 8,000 men, to attack fifty regiments and fifty squadrons — and Ugalde Carrillo still would not have found out until Sunday, July 26, at 5:15 a.m. I assure you that for every man who fought, twenty well-trained men were unable to fight for lack of weapons. When these young men marched along the streets of Havana in the student demonstration of the Martí Centennial, they solidly packed six blocks. If even 200 more men had been able to fight, or we had possessed twenty more hand grenades, perhaps this honorable court would have been spared all this inconvenience.

The politicians spend millions buying off consciences, whereas a handful of Cubans who wanted to save their country's honor had to face death barehanded for lack of funds. This shows how the country, to this very day, has been governed not by generous and dedicated men, but by political racketeers, the scum of our public life.

With the greatest pride I tell you that in accordance with our principles we have never asked a politician, past or present, for a penny. Our means were assembled with incomparable sacrifice. For example, Elpidio Sosa, who sold his job and came to me one day with 300 pesos "for the cause"; Fernando Chenard, who sold the photographic equipment with which he earned his living; Pedro Marrero, who contributed several months' salary and who had to be stopped from actually selling the very furniture in his house; Oscar Alcalde, who sold his pharmaceutical laboratory; Jesús Montané, who gave his five years' savings, and so on with many others, each giving the little he had.

One must have great faith in one's country to do such a thing. The memory of these acts of idealism brings me straight to the most bitter chapter of this defense — the price the tyranny made them pay for wanting to free Cuba from oppression and injustice.

Beloved corpses, you that once
Were the hope of my homeland,
Cast upon my forehead
The dust of your decaying bones!
Touch my heart with your cold hands!
Groan at my ears!
Each of my moans will
Turn into the tears of one more tyrant!
Gather around me! Roam about,
That my soul may receive your spirits
And give me the horror of the tombs
For tears are not enough
When one lives in infamous bondage!

Multiply the crimes of November 27, 1871, by ten and you will have the monstrous and repulsive crimes of July 26, 27, 28, and 29, 1953, in the province of Oriente. These are still fresh in our memory, but someday when years have passed, when the skies of the nation have cleared once more, when tempers have calmed and fear no longer torments our spirits, then we will begin to see the magnitude of this massacre in all its shocking dimension, and future generations will be struck with horror when they look back on these acts of barbarity unprecedented in our history. But I do not want to become enraged. I need clearness of mind and peace in my heavy heart in order to relate the facts as simply as possible, in no sense dramatizing them, but just as they took place. As a Cuban I am ashamed that heartless men should have perpetrated such unthinkable crimes, dishonoring our nation before the rest of the world.

9

The tyrant Batista was never a man of scruples. He has never hesitated to tell his people the most outrageous lies. To justify his treacherous coup of March 10, he concocted stories about a fictitious uprising in the army, supposedly scheduled to take place in April, and which he "wanted to avert so that the republic might not be drenched in blood." A ridiculous little tale nobody ever believed! And when he himself did want to drench the republic in blood, when he wanted to smother in terror and torture the just rebellion of Cuba's youth, who were not willing to be his slaves, then he contrived still more fantastic lies. How little respect one must have for a people when one tries to deceive them so miserably! On the very day of my arrest, I publicly assumed the responsibility for our armed movement of July 26. If there had been an iota of truth in even one of the many statements the dictator made against our fighters in his speech of July 27, it would have been enough to undermine the moral impact of my case. Why then, was I not brought to trial? Why were medical certificates forged? Why did they violate all procedural laws and ignore so scandalously the rulings of the court? Why were so many things done, things never before seen in a court of law, in order to prevent my appearance at all costs? In contrast, I could not begin to tell you all I went through in order to appear. I asked the court to bring me to trial in accordance with all established principles, and I denounced the underhanded schemes that were afoot to prevent it. I wanted to argue with them face to face. But they did not wish to face me. Who was afraid of the truth, and who was not?

The statements made by the dictator at Camp Columbia might be considered amusing if they were not so drenched in blood. He claimed we were a group of hirelings and that there were many foreigners among us. He said that the central part of our plan was an attempt to kill him — him, always him. As if the men who attacked the Moncada garrison could not have killed him and twenty like him if they had approved of such methods. He stated that our attack had been planned by ex-President Prío, and that it had been financed with Prío's money. It has been irrefutably proven that no link whatsoever existed between our movement and the last regime. He claimed that we had machine guns and hand grenades. Yet the military technicians have stated right here in this court that we only had one machine gun and not a single hand grenade. He said that we had beheaded the sentries. Yet death certificates and medical reports of all the army's casualties show not one death caused by the blade. But above all and most important, he said that we stabbed patients at the Military Hospital. Yet the doctors from that hospital — army doctors — have testified that we never even occupied the building, that no patient was either wounded or killed by us, and that the hospital lost only one employee, a janitor, who imprudently stuck his head out of an open window.

Whenever a chief of state, or anybody pretending to be one, makes declarations to the nation, he speaks not just to hear the sound of his own voice. He always has some specific purpose and expects some specific reaction, or has a given intention. Since our military defeat had already taken place, insofar as we no longer represented any actual threat to the dictatorship, why did they slander us like that? If it is still not clear that this was a blood-drenched speech, that it was simply an attempt to justify the crimes that they were perpetrating since the night before and that they were going to continue to perpetrate, then, let figures speak for me: On July 27, in his speech from the military headquarters, Batista said that the assailants suffered thirty-two dead. By the end of the week the number of dead had risen to more than eighty men. In what battles, where, in what clashes, did these young men die? Before Batista spoke, more than twenty-five prisoners had been murdered. After Batista spoke fifty more were massacred.

What a great sense of honor those modest army technicians and professionals had who did not distort the facts before the court, but gave their reports adhering to the strictest truth! These surely are soldiers who honor their uniform; these, surely, are men! Neither a real soldier nor a true man can degrade his code of honor with lies and crime. I know that many of the soldiers are indignant at the barbaric assassinations perpetrated. I know that they feel repugnance and shame at the smell of homicidal blood that impregnates every stone of Moncada garrison.

Now that he has been contradicted by men of honor within his own army, I defy the dictator to repeat his vile slander against us. I defy him to try to justify before the Cuban people his July 27 speech. Let him not remain silent. Let him speak. Let him say who the assassins are, who the ruthless, the inhumane. Let him tell us if the medals of honor, which he went to pin on the breasts of his heroes of that massacre, were rewards for the hideous crimes they had committed. Let him, from this very moment, assume his responsibility before history. Let him not pretend, at a later date, that the soldiers were acting without direct orders from him! Let him offer the nation an explanation for those seventy murders. The bloodshed was great. The nation demands it.

It is common knowledge that in 1933, at the end of the battle at the National Hotel, some of the officers were murdered after they had surrendered. *Bohemia* magazine protested energetically. It was also known that after the surrender of Fort Atarés, the besiegers' machine guns cut down a row of prisoners. And that one soldier, after asking who Blas Hernández was, blasted him with a bullet directly in the face and for this cowardly act was later promoted to the rank of officer. It is well known in Cuban history that assassination of prisoners was fatally linked with Batista's name. How naive we were, not to foresee this! However unjustifiable those killings of 1933 were, they took place in a matter of minutes, in no more time than it took for a round of machine-gun fire. What is more, they took place while tempers were still on edge.

This was not the case in Santiago de Cuba. Here all forms of ferocious outrages and cruelty were deliberately overdone. Our men were killed not in the course of a minute, an hour, or a day. Throughout an entire week the blows and tortures continued, men were thrown from rooftops and shot. All methods of extermination were incessantly practiced by well-skilled artisans of crime. Moncada garrison was turned into a workshop of torture and death. Some shameful individuals turned their uniforms into butchers' aprons. The walls were splattered with blood. The bullets imbedded in the walls were encrusted with singed bits of skin, brains and human hair, the grisly reminders of rifle shots fired full in the face. The grass around the barracks was dark and sticky with human blood. The criminal hands that are guiding the destiny of Cuba had written for the prisoners at the entrance of that den of death the very inscription of Hell: "Forsake all hope."

They did not even attempt to cover appearances. They did not bother in the least to conceal what they were doing. They thought they had deceived the people with their lies, and they ended up deceiving themselves. They felt themselves lords and masters of the universe, with power over life and death. So the fear they had experienced upon our attack at daybreak was dissipated in a feast of corpses, in a drunken orgy of blood.

Chronicles of our history, down through four and a half centuries, tell us of many acts of cruelty: the slaughter of defenseless Indians by the Spaniards; the plundering and atrocities of pirates along the coast; the barbarities of the Spanish soldiers during our war of independence; the shooting of prisoners of the Cuban army by the forces of Weyler; the horrors of the Machado regime; and so on through the bloody crimes of March 1935. But never has such a sad and bloody page been written in numbers of victims and in the viciousness of the victimizers, as in Santiago de Cuba. Only one man in all these centuries has stained with blood two separate periods of our history and has dug his claws into the flesh of two generations of Cubans. To release this river of blood, he waited for the centennial of the Apostle, just after the fiftieth anniversary of the republic, whose people fought for freedom, human rights, and happiness at the cost of so many lives. Even greater is his crime and even more condemnable because the man who perpetrated it had already, for eleven long years, lorded over his people — this people who, by such deep-rooted sentiment and tradition, loves freedom and repudiates evil. This man has furthermore never been sincere, loyal, honest, or chivalrous for a single minute of his public life.

He was not content with the treachery of January 1934, the crimes of March 1935, and the forty-million-dollar fortune that crowned his first regime. He had to add the treason of March 1952, the crimes of July 1953, and all the millions that only time will reveal. Dante divided his *Inferno* into nine circles. He put the criminals in the seventh, the thieves in the eighth, and the traitors in the ninth. Difficult dilemma the devils will be faced with, when they try to find an adequate spot for this man's soul — if this man has a soul. The man who instigated the atrocious acts in Santiago de Cuba doesn't even have a heart.

10

I know many details of the way in which these crimes were carried out, from the lips of some of the soldiers who, filled with shame, told me of the scenes they had witnessed.

When the fighting was over, the soldiers descended like savage beasts on Santiago de Cuba and they took the first fury of their frustrations out against the defenseless population. In the middle of a street, and far from the site of the fighting, they shot through the chest an innocent child who was playing by his doorstep. When the father approached to pick him up, they shot him through his head. Without a word they shot "Niño" Cala, who was on his way home with a loaf of bread in his hands. It would be an endless task to relate all the crimes and outrages perpetrated against the civilian population. And if the army dealt with those who had had no part at all in the action, you can imagine the terrible fate of the prisoners who had taken part or who were believed to have taken part. Just as, in this trial, they accused many people not at all involved in our attack, they also killed many prisoners who had no involvement whatsoever. The latter are not included in the statistics of victims released by the regime; those statistics refer exclusively to our men. Some day the total number of victims will be known.

The first prisoner killed was our doctor, Mario Muñoz, who bore no arms, wore no uniform, and was dressed in the white smock of a physician. He was a generous and competent man who would have given the same devoted care to the wounded adversary as to a friend. On the road from the Civilian Hospital to the barracks they shot him in the back and left him lying there, face down in a pool of blood. But the mass murder of prisoners did not begin until after three o'clock in the afternoon. Until this hour they awaited orders. Then Gen. Martín Díaz Tamayo arrived from Havana and brought specific instructions from a meeting he had attended with Batista, along with the head of the army, the head of the Military Intelligence Agency, and others. He said: "It is humiliating and dishonorable for the army to have lost three times as many men in combat as the insurgents did. Ten prisoners must be killed for each dead soldier." This was the order!

In every society there are men of base instincts. The sadists, brutes, conveyors of all the ancestral atavisms go about in the guise of human beings, but they are monsters, only more or less restrained by discipline and social habit. If they are offered a drink from a river of blood, they will not be satisfied until they drink the river dry. All these men needed was the order. At their hands the best and noblest Cubans perished: the most valiant, the most honest, the most idealistic. The tyrant called them mercenaries. There they were dying as heroes at the hands of men who collect a salary from the republic and who, with the arms the republic gave them to defend her, serve the interests of a clique and murder her best citizens.

Throughout their torturing of our comrades, the army offered them the chance to save their lives by betraying their ideology and falsely declaring that Prío had given them money. When they indignantly rejected that proposition, the army continued with its horrible tortures. They crushed their testicles and they tore out their eyes. But no one yielded. No complaint was heard nor favor asked. Even when they had been deprived of their virile organs, our men were still a thousand times more men than all their tormentors together. Photographs, which do not lie, show the bodies torn to pieces. Other methods were used. Frustrated by the valor of the men, they tried to break the spirit of our women. With a bleeding human eye in their hands, a sergeant and several other men went to the cell where our comrades Melba Hernández and Haydée Santamaría were held. Addressing the latter, and showing her the eye, they said: "This eye belonged to your brother. If you will not tell us what he refused to say, we will tear out the other." She, who loved her valiant brother above all things, replied full of dignity: "If you tore out an eye and he did not speak, much less will I." Later they came back and burned their arms with lit cigarettes until at last, filled with spite, they told the young Haydée Santamaría: "You no longer have a fiance because we have killed him too." But, still imperturbable, she answered: "He is not dead, because to die for one's country is to live forever." Never had the heroism and the dignity of Cuban womanhood reached such heights.

There wasn't even any respect for the combat wounded in the various city hospitals. There they were hunted down as prey pursued by vultures. In the Centro Gallego they broke into the operating room at the very moment when two of our critically wounded were receiving blood transfusions. They pulled them off the tables and, as the wounded could no longer stand, they were dragged down to the first floor where they arrived as corpses.

They could not do the same in the Spanish Clinic, where Gustavo Arcos and José Ponce were patients, because they were prevented by Dr. Posada who bravely told them they could enter only over his dead body.

Air and camphor were injected into the veins of Pedro Miret, Abelardo Crespo, and Fidel Labrador, in an attempt to kill them at the Military Hospital. They owe their lives to Captain Tamayo, an army doctor and a true soldier of honor, who, pistol in hand, wrenched them out of the hands of their merciless captors and transferred them to the Civilian Hospital. These five young men were the only ones of our wounded who survived.

In the early morning hours, groups of our men were removed from the barracks and taken in automobiles to Siboney, La Maya, Songo, and elsewhere. Then they were led out — tied, gagged, already disfigured by the torture —

and were murdered in isolated spots. They are recorded as having died in combat against the army. This went on for several days, and few of the captured prisoners survived. Many were compelled to dig their own graves. One of our men, while he was digging, wheeled around and slashed the face of one of his assassins with his pick. Others were even buried alive, their hands tied behind their backs. Many solitary spots became the graveyards of the brave. On the army target range alone, five of our men lie buried. Some day these men will be disinterred. Then they will be carried on the shoulders of the people to a place beside the tomb of Martí, and their liberated land will surely erect a monument to honor the memory of the martyrs of the centennial.

The last youth they murdered in the surroundings of Santiago de Cuba was Marcos Martí. He was captured with our comrade Ciro Redondo in a cave at Siboney on the morning of Thursday the thirtieth. These two men were led down the road, with their arms raised, and the soldiers shot Marcos Martí in the back. After he had fallen to the ground, they riddled him with bullets. Redondo was taken to the camp. When Major Pérez Chaumont saw him he exclaimed: "And this one? Why have you brought him to me?" The court heard of this incident from Redondo himself, the young man who survived thanks to what Pérez Chaumont called "the soldiers' stupidity."

It was the same throughout the province. Ten days after July 26, a newspaper in this city printed the news that two young men had been found hanged on the road from Manzanillo to Bayamo. Later the bodies were identified as those of Hugo Camejo and Pedro Véliz. Another extraordinary incident took place there: There were three victims — they had been dragged from Manzanillo barracks at two that morning. At a certain spot on the highway they were taken out, beaten unconscious, and left for dead. One of them, Andrés García, regained consciousness and hid in a farmer's house. Thanks to this the court learned the details of this crime too. Of all our men taken prisoner in the Bayamo area, this is the only survivor.

Near the Cauto River, in a spot known as Barrancas, at the bottom of a pit, lie the bodies of Raúl de Aguiar, Armando del Valle, and Andrés Valdés. They were murdered at midnight on the road between Alto Cedro and Palma Soriano by Sergeant Montes de Oca (in charge of the military post at Miranda barracks), Corporal Maceo, and the lieutenant in charge of Alto Cedro where the murdered men were captured.

In the annals of crime, Sergeant Eulalio González — better known as the "Tiger" of Moncada garrison — deserves a special place. Later this man didn't have the slightest qualms in bragging about his unspeakable deeds. It was he who with his own hands murdered our comrade Abel Santamaría. But that didn't satisfy him. One day as he was coming back from the Puerto Boniato Prison, where he raises pedigreed fighting cocks in the back courtyard, he got on a bus on which Abel's mother was also traveling. When this monster realized who she was, he began to brag about his grisly deeds, and — in a loud voice, so that the woman dressed in mourning could hear him — he said: "Yes, I have gouged many eyes out and I expect to continue gouging them out." The unprecedented moral degradation our nation is suffering is expressed beyond the power of words in that mother's sobs of grief before the cowardly insolence of the very man who murdered her son. When these mothers went to Moncada garrison to ask about their sons, it was with incredible cynicism and sadism that they were told: "Surely madam, you may see him at the Santa Ifigenia Hotel where we have put him up for you." Either Cuba is not Cuba, or the men responsible for these acts will have to face their reckoning one day. Heartless men, they threw crude insults at the people who bared their heads in reverence as the corpses of the revolutionaries were carried by.

There were so many victims that the government still

has not dared make public the complete list. They know their figures are false. They have all the victims' names, because prior to every murder they recorded all the vital statistics. The whole long process of identification through the National Identification Bureau was a huge farce, and there are families still waiting for word of their sons' fate. Why has this not been cleared up after three months?

I wish to state for the record here that all the victims' pockets were probed to the very last penny, and that all their personal effects, rings and watches, were stripped from their bodies and are brazenly being worn today by their assassins.

Honorable Judges, a great part of what I have just related you already know from the testimony of many of my comrades. But please note that many key witnesses have been barred from this trial, although they were permitted to attend the sessions of the previous trial. For example, I want to point out that the nurses of the Civilian Hospital are absent, even though they work in the same place where this hearing is being held. They were kept from this court so that, under my questioning, they would not be able to testify that — besides Dr. Mario Muñoz — twenty more of our men were captured alive. The regime fears that from the questioning of these witnesses some extremely dangerous testimony could find its way into the official transcript.

But Major Pérez Chaumont did appear here and he could not elude my questioning. What we learned from this man, a "hero" who fought only against unarmed and handcuffed men, gives us an idea of what could have been learned at the courthouse if I had not been isolated from the proceedings. I asked him how many of our men had died in his celebrated skirmishes at Siboney. He hesitated, I insisted, and he finally said twenty-one. Since I knew such skirmishes had never taken place, I asked him how many of our men had been wounded. He answered: "None. All of them were killed." It was then that I asked him, in astonishment, if the soldiers were using nuclear weapons. Of course, where men are shot point blank, there are no wounded. Then I asked him how many casualties the army had sustained. He replied that two of his men had been wounded. Finally I asked him if either of those two men had died, and he said no. I waited. Later, all of the wounded army soldiers filed by and it was discovered that none of them had been wounded at Siboney. This same Major Pérez Chaumont who hardly flinched at having assassinated twenty-one defenseless young men has built a palatial home in Ciudamar Beach. It's worth more than 100,000 pesos — his savings after only a few months under Batista's new rule. And if this is the savings of a major, imagine how much generals have saved!

11

Honorable Judges: Where are our men who were captured July 26, 27, 28, and 29? It is known that more than sixty men were captured in the area of Santiago de Cuba. Only three of them and the two women have been brought before the court. The rest of the accused were seized later. Where are our wounded? Only five of them are alive; the rest were murdered. These figures are irrefutable. On the other hand, twenty of the soldiers who we held prisoner have been presented here and they themselves have declared that they received not one offensive word from us. Thirty soldiers who were wounded, many in the street fighting, also appeared before you. Not one was killed by us. If the army suffered losses of nineteen dead and thirty wounded, how is it possible that we should have had eighty dead and only five wounded? Who ever witnessed a battle with twenty-one dead and no wounded, like these famous battles described by Pérez Chaumont?

We have here the casualty lists from the bitter fighting sustained by the invasion troops in the war of 1895, both in battles where the Cuban army was defeated and where it was victorious. The battle of Los Indios in Las Villas: twelve wounded, none dead. The battle of Mal Tiempo: four dead, twenty-three wounded. Calimete: sixteen dead, sixty-four wounded. La Palma: thirty-nine dead, eighty-eight wounded. Cacarajícara: five dead, thirteen wounded. Descanso: four dead, forty-five wounded. San Gabriel del Lombillo: two dead, eighteen wounded. In all these battles the number of wounded is twice, three times and up to ten times the number of dead, although in those days there were no modern medical techniques by which the percentage of deaths could be reduced. How then, now, can we explain the enormous proportion of sixteen deaths per wounded man, if not by the government's slaughter of the wounded in the very hospitals and by the assassination of the other helpless prisoners they had taken? The figures are irrefutable.

"It is shameful and a dishonor to the army to have lost three times as many men in combat as those lost by the insurgents; we must kill ten prisoners for each dead soldier." This is the concept of honor held by the petty corporals who became generals March 10. This is the code of honor they wish to impose on the national army. A false honor, a feigned honor, an apparent honor based on lies, hypocrisy, and crime; a mask of honor molded by those assassins with blood. Who told them that to die fighting is dishonorable? Who told them the honor of an army is the murdering of the wounded and the prisoners of war?

In wartime, armies that murder prisoners have always earned the contempt and abomination of the entire world. Such cowardice has no justification, even in a case where national territory is invaded by foreign troops. In the words of a South American liberator: "Not even the strictest military obedience may turn a soldier's sword into that of an executioner." The honorable soldier does not kill the helpless prisoner after the fight, but rather, respects him. He does not finish off a wounded man, but rather, helps him. He stands in the way of crime and, if he cannot prevent it, he acts as that Spanish captain who, upon hearing the shots of the firing squad that murdered Cuban students, indignantly broke his sword in two and refused to continue serving in that army.

The soldiers who murdered their prisoners were not worthy of the soldiers who died. I saw many soldiers fight with courage, for example, those in the patrols that fired their machine guns against us in almost hand-to-hand combat, or that sergeant who, defying death, rang the alarm to mobilize the barracks. Some of them live. I am glad. Others are dead. They believed they were doing their duty, and in my eyes this makes them worthy of admiration and respect. I deplore only the fact that valiant men should fall for an evil cause. When Cuba is freed, we should respect, shelter, and aid the wives and children of those courageous soldiers who perished fighting against us. They are not to blame for Cuba's miseries. They too are victims of this nefarious situation.

But what honor was earned by the soldiers who died in battle was lost by the generals who ordered prisoners to be killed after they surrendered. Men who became generals overnight, without ever having fired a shot; men who bought their stars with high treason against their country; men who ordered the execution of prisoners taken in battles in which they didn't even participate: these are the generals of March 10 — generals who would not even have been fit to drive the mules that carried the equipment in Antonio Maceo's army.

The army suffered three times as many casualties as we did. That was because our men were expertly trained, as the army men themselves have admitted, and also because we had prepared adequate tactical measures, another fact recognized by the army. The army did not perform brilliantly; despite the millions spent on espionage by the Military Intelligence Agency, they were totally taken by surprise, and their hand grenades failed to explode because they were obsolete. And the army owes all this to generals like Martín Díaz Tamayo and colonels like Ugalde Carrillo and Alberto del Río Chaviano. We were not seventeen traitors infiltrated into the ranks of the army, as was the case on March 10. Instead, we were 165 men who had traveled the length and breadth of Cuba to look death boldly in the face. If the army leaders had a notion of real military honor they would have resigned their commands rather than try to wash away their shame and incompetence in the blood of their prisoners.

To kill helpless prisoners and then declare that they died in battle: that is the military capacity of the generals of March 10. That was the way the worst butchers of Valeriano Weyler behaved in the cruelest years of our war of independence. The *Chronicles of War* include the following story: "On February 23, officer Baldomero Acosta entered Punta Brava with some cavalry when, from the opposite road, a squad of the Pizarro regiment approached, led by a sergeant known in those parts as *Barriguilla* (Pot Belly). The insurgents exchanged a few shots with Pizarro's men, then withdrew by the trail that leads from Punta Brava to the village of Guatao. Followed by another battalion of volunteers from Marianao and a company of troops from the Public Order Corps, who were led by Captain Calvo, Pizarro's squad of fifty men marched on Guatao. . . . As soon as their first forces entered the village they commenced their massacre — killing twelve of the peaceful inhabitants. . . . The troops led by Captain Calvo speedily rounded up all the civilians that were running about the village, tied them up, and took them as prisoners of war to Havana. . . . Not yet satisfied with their outrages, on the outskirts of Guatao they carried out another barbaric action killing one of the prisoners and horribly wounding the rest. The Marquis of Cervera, a cowardly and palatine soldier, informed Weyler of the pyrrhic victory of the Spanish soldiers; but Major Zugasti, a man of principles, denounced the incident to the government and officially called the murders perpetrated by the criminal Captain Calvo and Sergeant *Barriguilla* an assassination of peaceful citizens.

"Weyler's intervention in this horrible incident and his delight upon learning the details of the massacre may be palpably deduced from the official dispatch that he sent to the Ministry of War concerning these cruelties. 'Small regiment organized by Marianao's military commander with garrison troops fought and destroyed bands of Villanueva and Baldomero Acosta near Punta Brava, killing twenty of theirs, who were handed over to the Mayor of Guatao for burial, and taking fifteen prisoners, one of them wounded, and we assume more wounded were carried away by the enemy. One of ours suffered critical wounds, some suffered light bruises and wounds. Weyler.' "

What is the difference between Weyler's dispatch and that of Colonel Chaviano detailing the victories of Major Pérez Chaumont? Only that Weyler announces twenty dead and Chaviano, twenty-one. Weyler mentions one wounded soldier in his ranks. Chaviano mentions two. Weyler speaks of one wounded man and fifteen prisoners in the enemy's ranks. Chaviano records neither wounded men nor prisoners.

Just as I admire the courage of the soldiers who died bravely, I also admire the officers who bore themselves with dignity and did not drench their hands in this blood. Many of the survivors owe their lives to the commendable conduct of officers like Lieutenant Sarría, Lieutenant Campa, Captain Tamayo, and others, who were true gentlemen in their treatment of the prisoners. If men like these had not partially saved the name of the armed forces, it would be more honorable today to wear a dishrag than to wear an army uniform.

For my dead comrades, I claim no vengeance. Since their lives were priceless, the murderers could not pay for them even with their own lives. It is not by blood that we may redeem the lives of those who died for their country. The happiness of their people is the only tribute worthy of them.

What is more, my comrades are neither dead nor forgotten; they live today, more than ever, and their murderers will view with dismay the victorious spirit of their ideas rise from their corpses. Let the Apostle speak for me: "There is a limit to the tears we can shed at the graveside of the dead. Such limit is the infinite love for the homeland and its glory, a love that never falters, loses hope, nor grows dim. For the graves of the martyrs are the highest altars of our reverence."

When one dies
In the arms of a grateful country
Agony ends, prison chains break — and
At last, with death, life begins!

Up to this point I have confined myself almost exclusively to relating events. Since I am well aware that I am before a court convened to judge me, I will now demonstrate that all legal right was on our side alone, and that the verdict imposed on my comrades — the verdict now being sought against me — has no justification in reason, in social mores, or in terms of true justice.

I wish to be duly respectful to the Honorable Judges, and I am grateful that you find in the frankness of my plea no animosity towards you. My argument is meant simply to demonstrate what a false and erroneous position the judicial power has adopted in the present situation. To a certain extent, each court is nothing more than a cog in the wheel of this system and therefore must move along the course determined by the vehicle, although this by no means justifies any individual acting against his principles. I know very well that the oligarchy bears most of the blame. The oligarchy, without dignified protest, abjectly yielded to the dictates of the usurper and betrayed their country by renouncing the autonomy of the judicial power. Men who constitute noble exceptions have attempted to mend the system's mangled honor with their individual decisions. But the gestures of this minority have been of little consequence, drowned as they were by the obsequious and fawning majority. This fatalism, however, will not stop me from speaking the truth that supports my cause. My appearance before this court may be a pure farce in order to give a semblance of legality to arbitrary decisions, but I am determined to wrench apart with a firm hand the infamous veil that hides so much shamelessness. It is curious: the very men who have brought me here to be judged and condemned have never heeded a single decision of the court.

Since this trial may, as you said, be the most important trial since we achieved our national sovereignty, what I say here will perhaps be lost in the silence which the dictatorship has tried to impose upon me, but posterity will often turn its eyes to what you do here. Remember that today you are judging an accused man, but that you yourselves will be judged not once, but many times, as often as these days are submitted to scrutiny in the future. What I say here will then be repeated many times, not because it comes from my lips, but because the problem of justice is eternal and the people have a deep sense of justice above and beyond the hairsplitting of jurisprudence. The people wield simple but implacable logic, in conflict with all that is absurd and contradictory. Furthermore, if there is in this world a people that utterly abhors favoritism and inequality, it is the Cuban people. To them, justice is symbolized by a maiden with a scale and a sword in her hands. Should she cower before one group and furiously wield that sword against another group, then to the people of Cuba the maiden of justice will seem nothing more than a prostitute brandishing a dagger. My logic is the simple logic of the people.

12

Let me tell you a story: Once upon a time there was a republic. It had its constitution, its laws, its freedoms, a president, a congress, and courts of law. Everyone could assemble, associate, speak, and write with complete freedom. The people were not satisfied with the government officials at that time, but they had the power to elect new officials, and only a few days remained before they would do so. Public opinion was respected and heeded, and all problems of common interest were freely discussed. There were political parties, radio and television debates, and forums and public meetings. The whole nation pulsated with enthusiasm. This people had suffered greatly and, although it was unhappy, it longed to be happy and had a right to be happy. It had been deceived many times, and it looked upon the past with real horror. This country innocently believed that such a past could not return; the people were proud of their love of freedom, and they carried their heads high in the conviction that liberty would be respected as a sacred right. They felt confident that no one would dare commit the crime of violating their democratic institutions. They wanted a change for the better, aspired to progress; and they saw all this at hand. All their hope was in the future.

Poor country! One morning the citizens woke up dismayed. Under the cover of night, while the people slept, the ghosts of the past had conspired and had seized the citizenry by its hands, its feet, and its neck. That grip, those claws were familiar: those jaws, those death-dealing scythes, those boots. No; it was no nightmare; it was a sad and terrible reality: a man named Fulgencio Batista had just perpetrated the appalling crime that no one had expected.

Then a humble citizen of that people, a citizen who wished to believe in the laws of the republic, in the integrity of its judges, whom he had seen vent their fury against the underprivileged, searched through a social defense code to see what punishment society prescribed for the author of such a coup, and he discovered the following:

"Whosoever shall perpetrate any deed destined through violent means directly to change in whole or in part the constitution of the state or the form of the established government shall incur a sentence of six to ten years' imprisonment."

"A sentence of three to ten years' imprisonment shall be imposed upon the perpetrator of any act aimed at promoting an armed uprising against the constitutional powers of the state. The sentence shall be five to twenty years' imprisonment if the insurrection is carried out."

"Whosoever shall perpetrate an act with the specific purpose of preventing, in whole or in part, even temporarily, the Senate, the House of Representatives, the president, or the Supreme Court from exercising their constitutional functions will incur a sentence of from six to ten years' imprisonment."

"Whosoever shall attempt to impede or tamper with the normal course of general elections will incur a sentence of from four to eight years' imprisonment."

"Whosoever shall introduce, publish, propagate, or try to enforce in Cuba instructions, orders, or decrees that tend . . . to promote the unobservance of laws in force will incur a sentence of from two to six years' imprisonment."

"Whosoever shall assume command of troops, posts, fortresses, military camps, towns, warships, or military aircraft, without the authority to do so or without express government orders, will incur a sentence of from five to ten years' imprisonment."

"A similar sentence will be passed upon anyone who usurps the exercise of a function held by the constitution as properly belonging to the powers of state."

Without telling anyone, code in one hand and a deposition in the other, that citizen went to the old city building, that old building which housed the court competent and under obligation to bring cause against and punish those responsible for this deed. He presented a writ denouncing the crimes and asking that Fulgencio Batista and his seventeen accomplices be sentenced to 108 years in prison as decreed by the Social Defense Code; considering also aggravating circumstances of second offense, treachery, and acting under cover of night.

Days and months passed. What a disappointment! The accused remained unmolested: he strode up and down the country like a great lord and was called Honorable Sir and General: he removed and replaced judges at will. The very day the courts opened, the criminal occupied the seat of honor in the midst of our august and venerable patriarchs of justice.

Once more the days and the months rolled by, the people wearied of mockery and abuses. There is a limit to tolerance! The struggle began against this man who was disregarding the law; who had usurped power by the use of violence against the will of the people; who was guilty of aggression against the established order; tortured, murdered, imprisoned, and prosecuted those who had taken up the struggle to defend the law and to restore freedom to the people.

13

Honorable Judges: I am that humble citizen who one day demanded in vain that the courts punish the power-hungry men who had violated the law and torn our institutions to shreds. Now that it is I who am accused, for attempting to overthrow this illegal regime and to restore the legitimate constitution of the republic, I am held incommunicado for seventy-six days and denied the right to speak to anyone, even to my son. Between two heavy machine guns, I am led through the city. I am transferred to this hospital to be tried secretly with the greatest severity, and the prosecutor with the code in his hand solemnly demands that I be sentenced to twenty-six years in prison.

You will answer that on the former occasion the courts failed to act because force prevented them from doing so.

Well then, confess, this time force will compel you to condemn me. The first time you were unable to punish the guilty; now you will be compelled to punish the innocent. The maiden of justice twice raped.

And so much talk to justify the unjustifiable, to explain the inexplicable, and to reconcile the irreconcilable! The regime has reached the point of asserting that "might makes right" is the supreme law of the land. In other words, that using tanks and soldiers to take over the presidential palace, the national treasury, and the other government offices, and aiming guns at the heart of the people, entitles them to govern the people! The same argument the Nazis used when they occupied the countries of Europe and installed their puppet governments.

I heartily believe revolution to be the source of legal right; but the nocturnal armed assault of March 10 could never be considered a revolution. In everyday language, as José Ingenieros said, it is common to give the name of revolution to small disorders promoted by a group of dissatisfied persons in order to grab, from those in power, both the political sinecures and the economic advantages. The usual result is no more than a change of hands in the dividing up of jobs and benefits. This is not the criterion of a philosopher, as it cannot be that of a cultured man.

Leaving aside the problem of integral changes in the social system, not even on the surface of the public quagmire were we able to discern the slightest motion that could lessen the rampant putrefaction. The previous regime was guilty of petty politics, theft, pillage, and disrespect for human life; but the present regime has increased political skulduggery five-fold, pillage ten-fold, and a hundred-fold the lack of respect for human life.

It was known that *Barriguilla* had plundered and murdered; that he was a millionaire; that he owned in Havana a good many apartment houses, countless stock in foreign companies, fabulous accounts in American banks; that he agreed to divorce settlements to the tune of eighteen million pesos; that he was a frequent guest in the most lavishly expensive hotels for Yankee tycoons. But no one would ever think of *Barriguilla* as a revolutionary. *Barriguilla* is that sergeant of Weyler who assassinated twelve Cubans in Guatao. Batista's men murdered seventy in Santiago de Cuba. *De te fabula narratur* [History will be written about this].

Four political parties governed the country before March 10: the Authentic, Liberal, Democratic, and Republican parties. Two days after the coup, the Republican party gave its support to the new rulers. A year had not yet passed before the Liberal and Democratic parties were again in power: Batista did not restore the constitution, did not restore civil liberties, did not restore Congress, did not restore universal suffrage, did not restore in the last analysis any of the uprooted democratic institutions. But he did restore Verdeja, Guas Inclán, Salvito García Ramos, Anaya Murillo, and the top hierarchy of the traditional government parties — the most corrupt, rapacious, reactionary, and antediluvian elements in Cuban politics. So went the "revolution" of *Barriguilla!*

Lacking even the most elemental revolutionary content, Batista's regime represents in every respect a twenty-year regression for Cuba. Batista's regime has exacted a high price from all of us but primarily from the humble classes, which are suffering hunger and misery. Meanwhile the dictatorship has laid waste the nation with commotion, ineptitude, and anguish and now engages in the most loathsome forms of ruthless politics, concocting formula after formula to perpetuate itself in power, even if over a stack of corpses and a sea of blood.

Batista's regime has not set in motion a single nationwide program of betterment for the people. Batista delivered himself into the hands of the great financial interests. Little else could be expected from a man of his mentality — utterly devoid as he is both of ideals and of principles and utterly lacking the faith, confidence, and support of the masses. His regime merely brought with it a change of hands and a redistribution of the loot among a new group of friends, relatives, accomplices, and parasitical hangers-on that constitute the political retinue of the dictator. What great shame the people have been forced to endure so that a small group of egotists, altogether indifferent to the needs of their homeland, may find in public life an easy and comfortable modus vivendi.

How right Eduardo Chibás was in his last radio speech, when he said that Batista was encouraging the return of the colonels, castor oil, and the fugitive law! Immediately after March 10, Cubans again began to witness acts of veritable vandalism which they had thought banished forever from their nation. There was an unprecedented attack on a cultural institution: a radio station was stormed by the thugs of the Military Intelligence Agency, together with the young hoodlums of the Unitary Action Party, while broadcasting the "University of the Air" program. And there was the case of the journalist Mario Kuchilán, dragged from his home in the middle of the night and bestially tortured till he was nearly unconscious. There was the murder of student Rubén Batista and the criminal volleys fired at a peaceful student demonstration next to the wall where the Spanish volunteers shot the medical students in 1871.[7] And many cases like that of Dr. García Bárcena, where men coughed up blood in the courtrooms because of the barbaric tortures they received at the hands of the repressive security forces. I will not enumerate the hundreds of cases where groups of citizens have been brutally clubbed — men, women, children, and the aged. All of this was being done even before July 26.

Since then, as everyone knows, not even Cardinal Arteaga himself was spared such treatment. Everybody knows he was a victim of the repressive agents. According to the official story, he fell prey to a "band of thieves." For once the regime told the truth. For what else is this regime?

People have just contemplated with horror the case of

the journalist who was kidnapped and subjected to torture by fire for twenty days. Each new case brings forth evidence of unheard-of effrontery, of immense hypocrisy: the cowardice of those who shirk responsibility and invariably blame the enemies of the regime. Governmental tactics fit to be envied by the worst gangster mobs. Even the Nazi criminals were never so cowardly. Hitler assumed responsibility for the massacres of June 30, 1934, stating that for twenty-four hours he had been the German supreme court; the henchmen of this dictatorship — which defies all comparison because of its baseness, maliciousness, and cowardice — kidnap, torture, murder, and then loathsomely put the blame on the adversaries of the regime. Typical tactics of Sergeant *Barriguilla!*

Not once in all the cases I have mentioned, Honorable Judges, have the agents responsible for these crimes been brought to court to be tried for them. How is this? Was this not to be the regime of public order, peace, and respect for human life?

14

I have related all this in order to ask you now: Can this state of affairs be called a revolution, capable of formulating law and establishing rights? Is it or is it not legitimate to struggle against this regime? And must there not be a high degree of corruption in the courts of law when these courts imprison the citizens who try to rid their country of so much infamy?

Cuba is suffering from a cruel and base despotism. You are well aware that resistance to despots is legitimate. This is a universally recognized principle and our 1940 constitution expressly makes it a sacred right, in the second paragraph of Article 40: "It is legitimate to use adequate resistance to protect previously granted individual rights." And even if this prerogative had not been provided for by the supreme law of the land, it is a consideration without which one cannot conceive of the existence of a democratic collectivity. Professor Infiesta, in his book on constitutional law, differentiates between political and legal constitutions and states: "Sometimes the legal constitution includes constitutional principles which even without being so classified, would be equally binding solely on the basis of the people's consent, for example, the principle of majority rule or representation in our democracies." The right of insurrection in the face of the tyranny is one such principle, and whether or not it be included in the legal constitution it is always binding within a democratic society. The presentation of such a case to a high court is one of the most interesting problems of general law. Duguit has said in his *Treatise on Constitutional Law*: "If an insurrection fails, no court will dare rule that this unsuccessful insurrection was technically no conspiracy, no transgression against the security of the state, inasmuch as, the government being tyrannical, the intention to overthrow it was legitimate." But please take note: Duguit does not state, "the court ought not to rule." He says "no court will dare rule." More explicitly, he means that no court will dare, that no court will have enough courage to do so, under a tyranny. The issue admits no alternatives. If the court is courageous and does its duty, then yes, it will dare.

Recently there has been a violent controversy concerning the 1940 constitution. The Court of Social and Constitutional Rights ruled against it in favor of the so-called statutes. Nevertheless, Honorable Judges, I maintain that the 1940 constitution is still in force. My statement may seem absurd and extemporaneous to you. But do not be surprised. It is I who am astonished that a court of law should have attempted to deal a death blow to the legitimate constitution of the republic. Adhering strictly to facts, truth, and reason — as I have done all along — I will prove what I have just stated. The Court of Social and Constitutional Rights was instituted according to Article 172 of the 1940 constitution and the supplementary act of May 31, 1949.

These laws, by virtue of which the court was created, granted it, insofar as problems of unconstitutionality are concerned, a specific and clearly defined area of legal competence: to rule in all matters of appeals claiming the unconstitutionality of laws, legal decrees, resolutions, or acts that deny, diminish, restrain, or adulterate the constitutional rights and privileges or that jeopardize the operations of state agencies. Article 194 established very clearly the following: "All judges and courts are under the obligation to find solutions to conflicts between the constitution and the existing laws in accordance with the principle that the former shall always prevail over the latter." Therefore, according to the laws that created it, the Court of Social and Constitutional Rights should always rule in favor of the constitution. When this court caused the statutes to prevail over the constitution of the republic, it completely overstepped its boundaries and its established field of competence, thereby rendering a decision which is legally null and void. Furthermore, the decision itself is absurd, and absurdities have no validity in law nor in fact, not even from a metaphysical point of view. No matter how venerable a court may be, it cannot assert that circles are square or what amounts to the same thing, that the grotesque offspring of the April 4 statutes should be considered the official constitution of a state.

The constitution is understood to be the basic and supreme law of the nation, to define the country's political structure, regulate the functioning of government agencies, and determine the limits of their activities. It must be stable, enduring, and, to a certain extent, inflexible. The statutes fulfill none of these qualifications. To begin with, they harbor a monstrous, shameless, and brazen contradiction in regard to the most vital aspect of all this: the integration of the republican structure and the principle of national sovereignty. Article 1 reads: "Cuba is a sovereign and independent state constituted as a democratic republic." Article 2 reads: "Sovereignty resides in the will of the people, and all powers derive from this source." But then comes Article 118, which reads: "The president will be nominated by the cabinet." So it is not the people who choose the president, but rather the cabinet. And who chooses the cabinet? Article 120, section 13: "The president will be authorized to nominate and reappoint the members of the cabinet and to replace them when the occasion arises." So, after all, who nominates whom? Is this not the classic old problem of the chicken and the egg that no one has ever been able to solve?

One day eighteen hoodlums got together. Their plan was to assault the republic and loot its 350 million peso annual budget. Behind peoples' backs and with great treachery, they succeeded in their purpose. "Now what do we do next?" they wondered. One of them said to the rest: "You name me prime minister, and I'll make you generals." When this was done, he rounded up a group of twenty men and told them: "I will make you my cabinet if you make me president." In this way they named each other generals, ministers, and president, and then took over the treasury and the republic.

What is more, it was not simply a matter of usurping sovereignty at a given moment in order to name a cabinet, generals, and a president. This man ascribed to himself, through these statutes, not only absolute control of the nation, but also the power of life and death over every citizen — control, in fact, over the very existence of the nation. Because of this, I maintain that the position of the Court of Social and Constitutional Rights is not only treacherous, vile, cowardly, and repugnant, but also absurd.

The statutes contain an article which has not received much attention, but which gives us the key to this situation and is the one from which we shall derive decisive conclusions. I refer specifically to the modifying clause included in Article 257, which reads: "This constitutional law is open to reform by the cabinet with a two-thirds quorum vote." This is where mockery reaches its climax.

Not only did they exercise sovereignty in order to impose a constitution upon a people without that people's consent and to install a regime which concentrates all power in their own hands, but also, through Article 257, they assume the most essential attribute of sovereignty: the power to change the basic and supreme law of the land. And they have already changed it several times since March 10. Yet, with the greatest gall, they assert in Article 2 that sovereignty resides in the will of the people, and that the people are the source of all power. Since these changes may be brought about by a vote of two thirds of the cabinet, and the cabinet is named by the president, then the right to make and break Cuba is in the hands of one man; a man who is, furthermore, the most unworthy of all the creatures ever to be born in this land.

Was this then accepted by the Court of Social and Constitutional Rights? And is all that derives from it valid and legal? Very well, you shall see what was accepted: "This constitutional law is open to reform by the cabinet with a two-thirds quorum vote." Such a power recognizes no limits. Under its aegis, any article, any chapter, any section, even the whole law, may be modified. For example, Article 1, which I have just mentioned, says that Cuba is a sovereign and independent state constituted as a democratic republic, "although today it is in fact a bloody dictatorship." Article 3 reads: "The national boundaries include the island of Cuba, the Isle of Pines, and the neighboring keys . . . " and so on. Batista and his cabinet under the provisions of Article 257 can modify all these other articles. They can say that Cuba is no longer a republic but a hereditary monarchy, and he, Batista, can anoint himself king. He can dismember the national territory and sell a province to a foreign country as Napoleon did with Louisiana. He may suspend the right to life itself and, like Herod, order the decapitation of newborn children. All these measures would be legal, and you would have to incarcerate all those who opposed them, just as you now in-

tend to do with me. I have put forth extreme examples to
show how sad and humiliating our present situation is. To
think that all those absolute powers are in the hands of
men truly capable of selling our country along with all its
citizens!

As the Court of Social and Constitutional Rights has accepted this state of affairs, what more are they waiting for?
They may as well hang up their judicial robes. It is a fundamental principle of general law that there can be no constitutional statutes where the constitutional and legislative
powers reside in the same body. When the cabinet makes
the laws, the decrees, and the rules — and at the same time
has the power to change the constitution in a moment's
time — then I ask you: why do we need a Court of Social
and Constitutional Rights? The ruling in favor of this statute is irrational, inconceivable, illogical, and totally contrary to the republican laws that you, Honorable Judges,
swore to uphold. When the Court of Social and Constitutional Rights supported Batista's statutes against the constitution, the supreme law of the land was not abolished,
but rather the Court of Social and Constitutional Rights
placed itself outside the constitution, renounced its autonomy, and committed legal suicide. May it rest in peace!

15

The right to rebel, established in Article 40 of the constitution, is still valid. Was it established to function while
the republic was enjoying normal conditions? No. This
provision is to the constitution what a lifeboat is to a ship at
sea. The lifeboat is only launched when the ship has been
torpedoed by enemies lying in wait along its course. With
our constitution betrayed and the people deprived of all
their prerogatives, there was only one way open, one right
which no power may abolish: the right to resist oppression
and injustice. If any doubt remains, there is an article of
the Social Defense Code which the honorable prosecutor

would have done well not to forget. It reads, and I quote: "The appointed or elected government authorities that fail to resist sedition with all available means will be liable to a sentence of interdiction of from six to eight years." The judges of our nation were under the obligation to resist Batista's treacherous military coup of March 10. It is understandable that when no one has observed the law and when nobody else has done his duty, those who have observed the law and have done their duty should be sent to prison.

You will not be able to deny that the regime forced upon the nation is unworthy of Cuba's history. In his book, *The Spirit of Laws*, which is the foundation of the modern division of governmental power, Montesquieu makes a distinction between three types of government according to their basic nature: "the republican form wherein the whole people or a portion thereof has sovereign power; the monarchical form where only one man governs, but in accordance with fixed and well-defined laws; and the despotic form where one man without regard for laws nor rules acts as he pleases, regarding only his own will or whim." And then he adds: "A man whose five senses constantly tell him that he is everything and that the rest of humanity is nothing is bound to be lazy, ignorant, and sensuous." "As virtue is necessary to democracy, and honor to a monarchy, fear is of the essence to a despotic regime, where virtue is not needed and honor would be dangerous."

The right of rebellion against tyranny, Honorable Judges, has been recognized from the most ancient times to the present day by men of all creeds, ideas, and doctrines.

It was so in the theocratic monarchies of remote antiquity. In China it was almost a constitutional principle that when a king governed rudely and despotically he should be deposed and replaced by a virtuous prince.

The philosophers of ancient India upheld the principle

of active resistance to arbitrary authority. They justified revolution and very often put their theories into practice. One of their spiritual leaders used to say that "an opinion held by the majority is stronger than the king himself. A rope woven of many strands is strong enough to hold a lion."

The city-states of Greece and republican Rome not only admitted, but defended the meting-out of violent death to tyrants.

In the Middle Ages, John of Salisbury in his *Book of the Statesman* says that when a prince does not govern according to law and degenerates into a tyrant, violent overthrow is legitimate and justifiable. He recommends for tyrants the dagger rather than poison.

Saint Thomas Aquinas, in the *Summa Theologica*, rejects the doctrine of tyrannicide and yet upholds the thesis that tyrants should be overthrown by the people.

Martin Luther proclaimed that when a government degenerates into a tyranny that violates the laws, its subjects are released from their obligation to obey. His disciple, Philipp Melanchthon, upholds the right of resistance when governments become despotic. Calvin, the outstanding thinker of the Reformation with regard to political ideas, postulates that people are entitled to take up arms to oppose any usurpation.

No less a man than Juan de Mariana, a Spanish Jesuit during the reign of Philip II, asserts in his book, *De Rege et Regis Institutione,* that when a governor usurps power, or even if he were elected, when he governs in a tyrannical manner, it is licit for a private citizen to exercise tyrannicide, either directly or through subterfuge with the least possible disturbance.

The French writer, François Hotman, maintained that between rulers and subjects there is a bond or contract, and that the people may rise in rebellion against the tyranny of governments when the latter violate that pact.

About the same time, a booklet — which came to be

widely read — appeared under the title *Vindiciae Contra Tyrannos*, and it was signed with the pseudonym Stephanus Junius Brutus. It openly declared that resistance to governments is legitimate when rulers oppress the people and that it is the duty of honorable judges to lead the struggle.

The Scottish reformers John Knox and John Poynet upheld the same points of view. And, in the most important book of that movement, George Buchanan stated that if a government rules their destiny in an unjust and arbitrary fashion, then that government becomes a tyranny and can be divested of power or, in a final recourse, its leaders can be put to death.

Johannes Althus, a German jurist of the early seventeenth century, stated in his *Treatise on Politics* that sovereignty, as the supreme authority of the state, is born from the voluntary concourse of all its members; that governmental authority stems from the duty of obedience and justifies resistance or rebellion.

Thus far, Honorable Judges, I have mentioned examples from antiquity, from the Middle Ages, and from the beginnings of our times. I selected these examples from writers of all creeds. What is more, you can see that the right to rebellion is at the very root of Cuba's existence as a nation. By virtue of it you are today able to appear in the robes of Cuban judges. Would it be that those garments really served the cause of justice!

It is well known that in England during the seventeenth century two kings, Charles I and James II, were dethroned for despotism. These actions coincided with the birth of liberal political philosophy and provided the ideological base for a new social class, which was then struggling to break the bonds of feudalism. Against divine right autocracies, this new philosophy upheld the principle of the social contract and of the consent of the governed and constituted the foundation of the English revolution of 1688, the American revolution of 1775, and the French revolution of

1789. These great revolutionary events ushered in the liberation of the Spanish colonies in the New World — the final link in that chain being broken by Cuba. The new philosophy nurtured our own political ideas and helped us to evolve our Constitution of Guáimaro up to the constitution of 1940. The latter was influenced by the socialist currents of our time; the principles of the social function of property and of man's inalienable right to a decent living were built into it, although large vested interests have prevented full enforcement of those rights.

The right of insurrection against tyranny then underwent its final consecration and became a fundamental tenet of political liberty.

As far back as 1649, John Milton wrote that political power lies with the people, who can enthrone and dethrone kings and who have the duty of overthrowing tyrants.

John Locke, in his essay on government, maintained that when the natural rights of man are violated, the people have the right and the duty to alter or abolish the government. "The only remedy against unauthorized force is opposition to it by force."

Jean-Jacques Rousseau said with great eloquence in his *Social Contract:* "While a people sees itself forced to obey and obeys, it does well; but as soon as it can shake off the yoke and shakes it off, it does better, recovering its liberty through the use of the very right that has been taken away from it." "The strongest man is never strong enough to be master forever, unless he converts force into right and obedience into duty. Force is a physical power; I do not see what morality one may derive from its use. To yield to force is an act of necessity, not of will; at the very least, it is an act of prudence. In what sense could this be called a duty?" "To renounce freedom is to renounce one's status as a man, to renounce one's human rights, including one's duties. There is no possible compensation for renouncing everything. Total renunciation is incompatible with the nature of man and to take away all free will is to take away all moral conduct. In short, it is vain and contradictory to stipulate on the one hand an absolute authority and on the other an unlimited obedience."

Thomas Paine said that "one just man deserves more respect than a rogue with a crown."

The people's right to rebel has been opposed only by reactionaries like that clergyman of Virginia, Jonathan Boucher, who said: "The right to rebel is a censurable doctrine derived from Lucifer, the father of rebellions."

The Declaration of Independence of the Congress of Philadelphia, on July 4, 1776, consecrated this right in a beautiful paragraph which reads: "We hold these truths to be self-evident, that all men are created equal, that they are endowed by the Creator with certain inalienable rights, that among these are life, liberty, and the pursuit of happiness; That to secure these rights, governments are instituted among men, deriving their just powers from the consent of the governed; that whenever any form of government becomes destructive of these ends, it is the right of the people to alter or abolish it and to institute a new government, laying its foundation on such principles and organizing its powers in such form as to them shall seem most likely to effect their safety and happiness."

The famous French Declaration of the Rights of Man willed this principle to the coming generations: "When the government violates the rights of the people, insurrection is for them the most sacred of rights and the most imperative of duties." "When a person seizes sovereignty, he should be condemned to death by free men."

I believe I have sufficiently justified my point of view. I have called forth more reasons than the honorable prosecutor called forth to ask that I be condemned to twenty-six years in prison. All these reasons support men who struggle for the freedom and happiness of the people. None support those who oppress the people, revile them, and rob them heartlessly. Therefore I have been able to call forth many reasons and he could not adduce even one. How can Batista's presence in power be justified, when he gained it against the will of the people and by violating the laws of the republic through the use of treachery and force? How could anyone call legitimate a regime of blood, oppression, and ignominy? How could anyone call revolutionary a regime which has gathered the most backward men, methods, and ideas of public life around it? How could anyone consider legally valid the high treason of a court whose duty was to defend the constitution? With what right do the courts send to prison citizens who have tried to redeem their country by giving their own blood, their own lives? All this is monstrous in the eyes of the nation and to the principles of true justice!

Still there is one argument more powerful than all the others. We are Cubans and to be Cuban implies a duty; not to fulfill that duty is a crime, is treason. We are proud of the history of our country; we learned it in school and have grown up hearing of freedom, justice, and human rights. We were taught to venerate the glorious example of our heroes and martyrs. Céspedes, Agramonte, Maceo, Gómez, and Martí were the first names engraved in our minds. We were taught that the Titan once said that liberty is not begged for but won with the blade of a *machete*.[8] We were taught that for the guidance of Cuba's free citizens, the Apostle wrote in his book *The Golden Age*: "The man who abides by unjust laws and permits any man to trample and mistreat the country in which he was born is not an honorable man. . . . In the world there must be a certain degree of honor just as there must be a certain amount of light. When there are many men without honor, there are always others who bear in themselves the honor of many men. These are the men who rebel with great force against those who steal the people's freedom, that is to say, against those who steal human honor itself. In those men thousands more are contained, an entire people is contained, human dignity is contained." We were taught that

October 10 and February 24 are glorious anniversaries of national rejoicing because they mark days on which Cubans rebelled against the yoke of infamous tyranny. We were taught to cherish and defend the beloved flag of the lone star, and to sing every afternoon the verses of our National Anthem: "To live in chains is to live in opprobrium" and "to die for one's homeland is to live forever!" All this we learned and will never forget, even though today in our land there is murder and prison for the men who practice the ideas taught to them since the cradle. We were born in a free country that our parents bequeathed to us, and the island will sink into the sea before we consent to be slaves of anyone.

It seemed that the Apostle would die during his centennial. It seemed that his memory would be extinguished forever. So great was the affront! But he is alive; he has not died. His people are rebellious. His people are worthy. His people are faithful to his memory. There are Cubans who have fallen defending his doctrines. There are young men who in magnificent selflessness came to die beside his tomb, giving their blood and their lives so that he could keep on living in the heart of his nation. Cuba, what would have become of you had you let your Apostle die?

I come to the close of my defense plea but I will not end it as lawyers usually do, asking that the accused be freed. I cannot ask freedom for myself while my comrades are already suffering in the ignominious prison of the Isle of Pines. Send me there to join them and to share their fate. It is understandable that honest men should be dead or in prison in a republic where the president is a criminal and a thief.

To you, Honorable Judges, my sincere gratitude for having allowed me to express myself free from contemptible restrictions. I hold no bitterness towards you, I recognize that in certain aspects you have been humane and I know that the chief judge of this court, a man of impeccable private life, cannot disguise his repugnance at the current state of affairs that compels him to dictate unjust decisions. Still, a more serious problem remains for the Court of Appeals: the indictments arising from the murder of seventy men, that is to say, the greatest massacre we have ever known. The guilty continue at liberty and with weapons in their hands — weapons which continually threaten the lives of all citizens. If all the weight of the law does not fall upon the guilty, because of cowardice or because of domination of the courts, and if then all the judges do not resign, I pity you your honor. And I regret the unprecedented shame that will fall upon the judicial power.

I know that imprisonment will be harder for me than it has ever been for anyone, filled with cowardly threats and hideous cruelty. But I do not fear prison, as I do not fear the fury of the miserable tyrant who took the lives of seventy of my comrades. Condemn me. It does not matter. History will absolve me.

Notes

1. The "Master" is a reference to José Martí.
2. March 10, 1952, was the date of Batista's coup d'etat.
3. *Mambises* were Cuban independence fighters during the first war of independence.
4. On October 10, 1868, Céspedes proclaimed the independence of Cuba with the "Cry of Yara." On February 2, 1895, Cuba's second war of independence was launched with the "Cry of Baire."
5. One *caballería* is equal to about 33 acres.
6. The "Apostle" is a reference to José Martí.
7. On October 27, 1871, eight medical students at the University of Havana were executed, charged with desecrating the graves of Spanish colonial representatives.
8. The "Titan" is a reference to Antonio Maceo.

Chronology

March 10, 1952	Fulgencio Batista seizes power in coup d'etat
July 26, 1953	Attack on Moncada garrison
October 16, 1953	Fidel Castro appears before Emergency Tribunal, delivers speech
February 20, 1954	Haydée Santamaría and Melba Hernández released from prison
October 1954	"History Will Absolve Me" begins distribution in Cuba
February 24, 1955	Batista begins "legal" term, announces elections within two years
May 15, 1955	Fidel Castro and other veterans of Moncada released from Isle of Pines prison
July 1955	Fidel Castro leaves Cuba for Mexico
August 16, 1955	First July 26 Movement manifesto from exile is distributed
March 19, 1956	Fidel Castro breaks with Orthodox Party leaders
September 1956	Mexico Pact establishes alliance between July 26 Movement and Revolutionary Directorate
December 2, 1956	Landing of the *Granma* in Cuba
March 13, 1957	Attack by Revolutionary Directorate on presidential palace
July 12, 1957	Sierra Manifesto sets out basis for broad, united revolutionary front to overthrow Batista
September 1957	Miami Pact forms National Liberation Junta; repudiated publicly by Castro December 14, 1957
April 9, 1958	General strike fails
May 24, 1958	Batista launches all-out military offensive against Rebel Army in Sierra Maestra
July 11-20, 1958	Battle of El Jigüe; decisive Rebel Army victory marks beginning of counteroffensive
July 20, 1958	Caracas Pact, initiated by July 26 Movement, unites broad spectrum of forces in support of a civilian-revolutionary front
January 1, 1959	Batista flees; general strike; revolution triumphs

Index

Further reading on the
Cuban revolution

Episodes of the Cuban Revolutionary War, 1956–58

Ernesto Che Guevara

A firsthand account of the military campaigns and political events that culminated in the January 1959 popular insurrection that overthrew the U.S.-backed dictatorship in Cuba. With clarity and humor, Guevara discribes his own political education. He explains how the struggle transformed the men and women of the Rebel Army and July 26 Movement led by Fidel Castro. And how these combatants forged a political leadership capable of guiding millions of workers and peasants to open the socialist revolution in the Americas. $23.95

In Defense of Socialism

Fidel Castro

Four Speeches on the 30th Anniversary of the Cuban Revolution, 1988-89

Not only is economic and social progress possible without the dog-eat-dog competition of capitalism, Castro argues, but socialism remains the only way forward for humanity. Castro also discusses the revolutionary struggle that brought down the Batista dictatorship in January 1959. $13.95

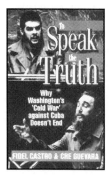

To Speak the Truth

Why Washington's 'Cold War' against Cuba Doesn't End

Fidel Castro and Che Guevara

In historic speeches before the United Nations and its bodies, Guevara and Castro address the workers of the world, explaining why the U.S. government is determined to destroy the example set by the socialist revolution in Cuba and why its effort will fail. $16.95

The Bolivian Diary of Ernesto Che Guevara

Guevara's account of the 1966–67 guerrilla struggle in Bolivia. A day-by-day chronicle of the campaign to forge a continent-wide revolutionary movement of workers and peasants capable of seizing state power. Includes excerpts from the diaries and accounts of other combatants, including—for the first time in English—*My Campaign with Che* by Bolivian leader Inti Peredo. Introduction by Mary-Alice Waters. $21.95

'I Shall Be a Marxist-Leninist to the End of My Life'

Fidel Castro

In this 1961 speech, Castro explains why only a socialist revolution could bring about the profound social changes Cuban working people were facing down Washington to achieve. In *Selected Speeches of Fidel Castro*. 8½ x 11 format $14.00

The Second Declaration of Havana

In 1962, as the example of Cuba's socialist revolution spread throughout the Americas, the workers and farmers of Cuba issued their uncompromising call for continent-wide revolutionary struggle. Booklet $4.50

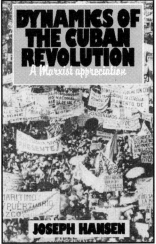

Dynamics of the Cuban Revolution

A Marxist Appreciation
Joseph Hansen

How did the Cuban revolution come about? Why does it represent, as Joseph Hansen put it, an "unbearable challenge" to U.S. imperialism? What political challenges has it confronted? Written with polemical clarity as the revolution advanced. $20.95

Also from Pathfinder

The Changing Face of U.S. Politics

Working-Class Politics and the Trade Unions

JACK BARNES

A handbook for workers coming into the factories, mines, and mills, as they react to the uncertain life, ceaseless turmoil, and brutality of capitalism in the closing years of the twentieth century. It shows how millions of workers, as political resistance grows, will revolutionize themselves, their unions, and all of society. $19.95

Lenin's Final Fight

Speeches and Writings, 1922–23

V. I. LENIN

The record of Lenin's last effort to win the leadership of the Communist Party of the USSR in the early 1920s to maintain the political course that had enabled the workers and peasants of the old tsarist empire to carry out the first successful soviet revolution and begin building a world communist movement. The issues posed in that battle remain at the heart of world politics today. Includes several items appearing in English for the first time. $19.95

Cosmetics, Fashions, and the Exploitation of Women

JOSEPH HANSEN, EVELYN REED, AND MARY-ALICE WATERS

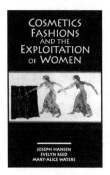

How big business promotes cosmetics to generate profits and perpetuate the oppression of women. In her introduction, Mary-Alice Waters explains how the entry of millions of women into the workforce during and after World War II irreversibly changed U.S. society and laid the basis for a renewed rise of struggles for women's equality. $12.95

The Leninist Strategy of Party Building

The Debate on Guerrilla Warfare in Latin America

JOSEPH HANSEN

In the 1960s and '70s, revolutionists in the Americas and throughout the world debated how to apply the lessons of the Cuban revolution to struggles elsewhere. An analysis by the leading participant in that debate. $26.95

Teamster Rebellion

FARRELL DOBBS

The 1934 strikes that built an industrial union and a fighting social movement in Minneapolis, recounted by a leader of that battle. The first in a four-volume series on the Teamster-led strikes and organizing drives in the Midwest that helped pave the way for the CIO and pointed a road toward independent labor political action. Also available in French. $16.95

The History of the Russian Revolution

LEON TROTSKY

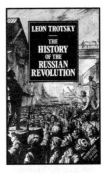

The social, economic, and political dynamics of the first socialist revolution. The story is told by one of the revolution's principal leaders writing from exile in the early 1930s, with these historic events still fresh in his mind. Also available in Russian. Unabridged edition, 3 vols. in one. 1358 pp. $35.95

Malcolm X Speaks

"No, I'm not an American. I'm one of the 22 million Black people who are victims of Americanism." The best selection of speeches and statements from the last year of Malcolm's life. $17.95

The Politics of Chicano Liberation

EDITED BY OLGA RODRIGUEZ

Draws on the lessons of the rise of the Chicano movement in the United States in the 1960s and 70s, which dealt a lasting blow against the oppression of the Chicano people and the divisions within the working class based on language and national origin. Presents a fighting program for those who are today determined to defend hard-won social conquests and build a revolutionary movement capable of leading humanity out of the wars, racist assaults, and social crisis of capitalism in its decline. $13.95

The Communist Manifesto

KARL MARX, FREDERICK ENGELS

Founding document of the modern working-class movement, published in 1848. Explains why communists act on the basis not of preconceived schemas but of *facts,* as participants in the ongoing class struggle. And why communism, to the degree it is a theory, is the generalization of the historical line of march of the working class and the political conditions for its liberation. Also available in Spanish and French. Booklet $3.95

The Revolution Betrayed

What Is the Soviet Union and Where Is It Going?

LEON TROTSKY

Classic study of the Soviet workers state and its degeneration under the brutal domination of the privileged social caste whose spokesman was Stalin. Illuminates the roots of the Russian crisis of the 1990s. Also available in Spanish. $19.95

On the Paris Commune

KARL MARX AND FREDERICK ENGELS

"Storming heaven," Marx wrote, the "proletariat for the first time held political power" in Paris for three months in 1871 and the international workers struggle "entered upon a new stage." Writings, letters, and speeches on the Paris Commune. $15.95

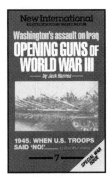

Defending Cuba, Defending Cuba's Socialist Revolution

MARY-ALICE WATERS

In face of the greatest economic difficulties in the history of the revolution, Cuba's workers and farmers are defending their political power, their independence and sovereignty, and the historic course they set out on more than 35 years ago. Mary-Alice Waters explains why in *New International* no. 10. Together with "Imperialism's March toward Fascism and War" by Jack Barnes. $14.00

Opening Guns of World War III

Washington's Assault on Iraq

JACK BARNES

The U.S. government's murderous assault on Iraq heralded increasingly sharp conflicts among imperialist powers, the rise of rightist and fascist forces, growing instability of international capitalism, and more wars. In *New International* no. 7. Also includes "Communism, the Working Class, and Anti-Imperialist Struggle" by Samad Sharif. $12.00

Che Guevara, Cuba, and the Road to Socialism

Articles by Ernesto Che Guevara, Carlos Rafael Rodríguez, Carlos Tablada, Mary-Alice Waters, Steve Clark, Jack Barnes. Exchanges from the early 1960s and from today on the relevance of the political and economic perspectives defended by Ernesto Che Guevara. In *New International* no. 8. Also available in Spanish. $10.00

The Rise and Fall of the Nicaraguan Revolution

The achievements and worldwide impact of the workers and farmers government that came to power in Nicaragua in 1979, and the political retreat of the Sandinista National Liberation Front leadership that led to the downfall of this government in the closing years of the 1980s. In *New International* no. 9. $14.00

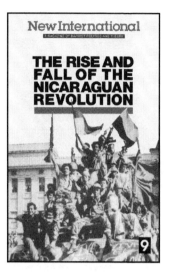

Communism and the Fight for a Popular Revolutionary Government

MARY-ALICE WATERS

Examines the concrete lessons from the revolutions of 1848, through the Paris Commune and Russian revolution, to the Cuban revolution. Traces the struggles of the working-class movement to take political power; establish a popular revolutionary government; and use this state power to uproot capitalism while beginning the transition to a new social and economic order. In *New International* no. 3. $8.00

The Coming Revolution in South Africa

JACK BARNES

The one-person, one-vote elections in 1994 and victory of the African National Congress, was a historic step in the democratic revolution. This article explores the social roots of apartheid in South African capitalism and the tasks of the toilers in dismantling the legacy of inequality. Only among the most committed cadres of this ANC-led struggle, Barnes writes, can the working class begin forging a communist leadership. In *New International* no. 5. $9.00

Most of these articles are also available in Spanish in *Nueva Internacional*, and in French in *Nouvelle Internationale*. Some are also available in Swedish in *Ny International*.

Distributed by Pathfinder